Modernity

Religious and Ethical Perspectives

Nicos Mouzelis

Modernity

Religious and Ethical Perspectives

Nicos Mouzelis

First published in 2021
as part of the *Religion in Society* Book Imprint
doi:10.18848/978-1-86335-252-9/CGP (Full Book)

Common Ground Research Networks
60 Hazelwood Drive
University of Illinois Research Park
Champaign, IL
61820

Copyright © Nicos Mouzelis 2021

All rights reserved. Apart from fair dealing for the purposes of study, research, criticism or review as permitted under the applicable copyright legislation, no part of this book may be reproduced by any process without written permission from the publisher.

Library of Congress Cataloging-in-Publication Data

Names: Mouzelis, Nicos P., author.
Title: Modernity : religious and ethical perspectives / by Nicos Mouzelis.
Description: Champaign, IL : Common Ground Research Networks, 2021. | Includes bibliographical references and index. | Summary: "An examination of the three unique structural features of modern societies: inclusion of the whole population into the nation state, top-down differentiation of institutional spheres and the expansion of individualisation from the top to the base of the social pyramid. The author shows how the above features relate to present day religious phenomena such as secularisation/desecularisation, the new religious movements and the forms of present day spiritualities. He examines the extent to which secularisation and rationalisation led to the "disenchantment of the world". Later, however, one observes a reaction to the established, hierarchically organised churches and to the adherence, mainly of young people, to less structured religious groups, to religious syncretism and to individual seekers who tried to find "their own God". From this perspective, one can argue that we have a partial "re-enchantment of the world""-- Provided by publisher.
Identifiers: LCCN 2021023834 (print) | LCCN 2021023835 (ebook) | ISBN 9781863352529 (hardback) | ISBN 9781863352536 (paperback) | ISBN 9781863352543 (adobe pdf)
Subjects: LCSH: Religion and civilization. | Civilization, Modern. | Civilization, Modern--Moral and ethical aspects.
Classification: LCC BL55 .M68 2021 (print) | LCC BL55 (ebook) | DDC 306.6--dc23
LC record available at https://lccn.loc.gov/2021023834
LC ebook record available at https://lccn.loc.gov/2021023835

Cover Photo Credit: *Ancient of Days Setting a Compass to the Earth* (1794) illustration from Europe: a Prophecy by William Blake (1752-1827). Original from The New York Public Library. Digitally enhanced by rawpixel

Table of Contents

Introduction 1

Chapter 1 3
Modernity
    On the Unique Features of Modernity
    Present Day Globalised Modernity: Late Modern or Post-Modern?
    Modernity or Modernities?

Chapter 2 17
Modernity: Religious Trends
    Massive Inclusion into the National Centre: The Process of Religious Rationalization
    Top-Down Differentiation of Institutional Spheres: The Issue of Secularization
    Overall Individualization: The New Spiritualities

Chapter 3 33
Modernity: The Fundamentalist Dimension
    On the Specifity of the Fundamentalist Phenomenon

Chapter 4 45
Modernity and Ethical Issues:
MacIntyre's Three Moral Discourses
    A Brief Exposé of MacIntyre's Theory

Chapter 5 59
Self and Self-Other Reflexivity
    Reflexivity: Apophatic and Cataphatic

Chapter 6 71
Instead of a Conclusion
Modernity: Six Orientations to the Divine

Appendix I 79
Lacan and Meditation:
From the Symbolic to the Postsymbolic

Appendix II...85
Decision Making and the Meditative Subject:
A Fourfold Typology

References 95

Index 102

Acknowledgments

For Thalia

Introduction

The book's main aim is to explore the linkages between the sociostructural features of post-traditional modern societies and some key developments in the religious, spiritual and ethical spheres. From this perspective, the focus is less on description and more on a theoretically oriented attempt to show the elective affinity between religious trends and the type of social organization which became dominant in the west during the English industrial revolution and the 1789 political revolution in France.

The first chapter analyses the notion of modernity, a notion which plays a central role in the social sciences today. Modernity in *sociostructural* rather than *cultural* terms entails three major characteristics: the gradual demise of the non-differentiated traditional community and the massive inclusion of a population to the "imaginary community" of the nation state. It also entails the top down, overall differentiation of institutional spheres and the large scale spread of individualization. The second chapter examines in a more specific manner the complex links between the structural features of modernity and such religious developments as the weakening of the traditional divide between popular and rationalised religious forms, the dialectic between secularization and desecularization processes, and the rise of new religious movements. The third chapter examines religious fundamentalism and its link to modernity's social organisation.

In the following three chapters I examine ethical theories which, more or less directly, are linked with the modernity concept. As it is well known, ethical relativism which is widely spread in modernity, stresses that there are no eternal codes that are valid in a transhistorical manner. In dealing with the relativism-anti-relativism debate, in Chapter IV I critique MacIntyre's well known theory which attempts to overcome ethical relativism by linking ethical norms and values to his notion of tradition. Against the above, in Chapter V, I discuss two theories (that of Buber and Krishnamurti) which reject all attempts to provide ethical foundations via tradition, sacred texts, scientific or philosophical analysis. For both authors, the ethical emerges spontaneously in the context of a special relationship between self and the other.

Finally, in Instead of Conclusion, I examine six basic orientations to the divine: theism, religious anthropocentrism, religious syncretism, apatheism, agnosticism and atheism. I try to show briefly how the above orientations change in the modern era. In all six chapters the focus is not on theological debates or on the history of religions old or new. It is rather to show the elective affinity and concrete linkages between religious trends and modernity's basic structural features.

There are also two appendixes. In the first I focus on meditation, a practice which spreads rapidly in late modernity. More specifically, I explore its relationship with Lacan's theory of language and the symbolic. I argue that to the extent that the main aim of most meditative methods is to bracket language, thoughts and words for a certain period of time, we can view this process as a passage from the Lacanian presymbolic and symbolic to a postsymbolic level. As to the second appendix, it tries to link decision making theories with four modes arriving at a decision, one of which is linked to meditation.

Finally, four of the book's eight texts (Chapter II, IV, V and Appendix I) have already been published[*]. In order to enhance the overall unity of the text, I have slightly altered parts of the already published articles. It is for the same reasons that very short passages of previous chapters are repeated in a somewhat different form in following chapters.

---

[*] Chapter II: (2012), "Modernity and the Secularization Debate", *Sociology*, Vol. 46, No. 2, pp. 207-223; Chapter IV: (2011), "Encyclopaedia, Genealogy, Tradition: A Sociocultural Critique of Macintyre's Three Moral Discourses", *The Sociological Review*, Vol. 59, No. 1, pp. 1-16; Chapter V: (2010),"Self And Self-Other Reflexivity: The Apophatic Dimension", *European Journal of Social Theory*, Vol. 13, No. 2, pp. 271-284 and (2010), "Ethical and Spiritual Anti-Foundationalism: Buber, Levinas, Krishnamurti", *Social Theory: An International Journal of Social and Political Theory*, Vol. 1, pp. 9-31; Appendix I: (2014), "Lacan and Meditation: From the Symbolic to the Postsymbolic?", *Psychoanalysis, Culture & Society*, Vol. 19, No. 2, pp. 127-136.

Chapter 1

Modernity

The concept of modernity as all key concepts in the social sciences is polysemic. It has different meanings according to the theoretical context within which it operates. Given this, a fruitful way of exploring its various dimensions is to see how it is used by social theorists who try to tackle issues related to our recent past and present predicament. I will deal with three interrelated issues:

i. Whether or not it is possible to identify unique features of modernity, i.e., features which do not exist in traditional pre-modern societies.

ii. Whether the social structure and culture of developed societies which are linked to the neo-liberal globalization should be labelled "late-modern" or "post-modern".

iii. Whether one should identify modernity with the liberal democratic capitalist order, or whether one should consider the above type of social order as one among other, different modernities.

On the Unique Features of Modernity

What is specific about modernity? Are there any unique features which one can call modern? Usually one tries to answer such questions by focusing less on social structural traits and more on socio-cultural ones; such as the enlightenment belief in rationality overcoming obscurantism and religious dogmatism, the emphasis on science bringing about material progress, radical doubt, atheism, nihilism, hybridization, individualism, enhanced reflexivity etc.

Now it seems to me that all the above features are not unique to modernity, in the sense that one can find similar features, although not dominant, in pre-modern social orders. If one looks for instance at such belief systems as materialism, atheism, deism etc., one finds them not only in the European enlightenment and post-enlightenment period but also in a number of pre-Socratic and post-Socratic ancient greek and roman philosophers and their disciples[1]. And the same is true if one focuses on socio-cultural or psycho-cultural phenomena such as

---

[1] On Greco-roman materialism and atheism, see Minois 1998.

individualism, atomization, cosmopolitanism, existential angst, ambiguity, nostalgia etc. In the large Hellenistic urban centres of Alexandria, Antioch and Rhodes for instance, particularly among the elites, one can find similar features[2]. What gives to the late-modern or post-modern features their uniqueness is their linkage to a type of social organization which, as already mentioned, became dominant in the West after the English industrial and French political revolutions. Such an organization portrays three social structural features which are unique i.e., which one does not find in even the most complex pre-modern societies. These are:

- The decline of segmental localism and the mobilisation/inclusion of the population into the national centre.

- The top-down differentiation of institutional spheres.

- Widespread individualization.

Decline of Segmental Localism and Inclusion of the Population into the National Centre

Employing Durkheimian terminology, one can argue that pre-modern, traditional communities had a non-differentiated, segmental social organization. In this respect they were self-sufficient, relatively autonomous *vis-à-vis* more inclusive social units. In the west, this localist, self-containment/autonomy was first undermined by the absolutist model of governance which took its more developed form in Louis XIV France[3]. Given technological developments in the military sphere and inter-state competition at the time, the absolutist model, although challenged in seventeenth century England, spread widely in continental Europe[4,] thus paving the way for the large-scale dominance of the nation-state in the nineteenth and twentieth centuries. This, in combination with the dominance of

---

[2] See Ferguson 1969: 33ff. By this argument I do not want to imply that all cultural features of modernity can be found in pre-modern social formations. For instance, quite obviously, postmodern cultural features linked to technological developments (e.g., video art, simulacra, the fascination with mediated images) do not exist in pre-modernity.

[3] The French monarchy and its administration, as it was finally shaped under Louis XIV, was the prototype of European absolutist rule, a model imitated all over Europe. Up to the seventeenth century the French nobility managed to maintain some of its political functions by exercising constitutional opposition to the crown through the Estates General, and the local *parlements*. But the Bourbons, unlike the English Kings, gradually managed to reduce its local power. The provincial governing positions ceased to be the hereditary fiefs of the nobility and the autonomy of the local *parlements* was destroyed, their powers being regulated by the Royal Council. The famous *intendants*, the crown representatives to the provinces, first appeared in the sixteenth century. With their powers extended by Richelieu, they gradually managed to weaken aristocratic self-government till they became the effective masters of all local affairs. See Clark 1969: 176-197.

[4] For the spread of the absolutist state, see P. Anderson 1974.

industrial capitalism[5] at about the same period, led to the gradual decline of segmental localism and the unprecedented large-scale mobilisation and inclusion of the population into the wider economic, political, social, and cultural arenas of the nation-state.

The above "drawing-in" process can be thought of as a vast shift of human and non-human resources from the periphery to the national centre. From an *actor/agency* perspective it can be conceptualized as a process of concentration at the top of not only the means of economic production, but also those of violence/domination, as well as those of influence or cultural production. As the local economic producers, political potentates, and virtuosi of particularistic rituals and narratives were losing control and/or ownership of their means of economic, political and cultural production, there emerged not only a concentration of power in the hands of national elites, but also a shift in people's identifications and attachments from the local communities to the symbols and ideologies of what B. Anderson (1991) has called the "imagined community" of the nation-state.

What made this massive process of drawing into the centre possible was initially the extraordinary expansion of the state's administrative and surveillance mechanisms. In fact, the nation-state, by using newly developed bureaucratic and military technologies managed to penetrate into the periphery to a degree unknown to any pre-modern, pre-industrial social formation, however complex or despotic[6].

Finally, the massive inclusion into the centre which entails deep state penetration can take both autonomous and heteronomous forms. In the former case civic, political and socioeconomic rights spread gradually "downwards", this resulting into a strong civil society (e.g., 19th and 20th century Britain). In the heteronomous case people were brought into the centralized administrative, military and cultural mechanisms of the nation state but without the granting of political rights (the case of 19th century Prussia).

Top-Down Differentiation of Institutional Spheres

The decline of localism and the massive mobilisation/inclusion into the national centre was not merely a quantitative move from the small to the large. In *systemic* terms, the drawing in process took place in a context of rapid and thorough

---

[5] For the great transformative power of industrial capital, see Dobb 1968.
[6] For the development of such technologies which enhanced the "infrastructural powers" of the state, see Mann 1992. It is worth mentioning here that the motor force from pre-modernity to the creation of the nation state had initially less an economic and more an administrative/political character. Given the 17th century scientific revolution and the subsequent development of formidable military and organizational technologies we see, particularly during the Napoleonic period, the creation of mass armies. Mass armies require resources which only a highly "penetrative" state apparatus could extract from its subjects. These developments preceded the dominance of industrial capitalism in the late 19th century (Tilly 1975). To put it in terms of our definition of modernity mass inclusion into the political arena preceded the inclusion into the national economic sphere.

differentiation as institutional spheres (economic, political, social, cultural) started portraying their own logic, their own reproductive technologies, their own historical trajectories.

Structural-functional differentiation is not, of course, unique to modernity. Complex pre-industrial social formations such as empires also portray a considerable degree of differentiation. But as Marx (1859) and others have pointed out, in such societies this process is limited to the top. The differentiated parts or subsystems of the centre are superimposed on the non-differentiated, segmentally organised peripheries. This means that the degree of penetration of the centralized economic, political and cultural apparatuses is both very weak and highly uneven (Mann 1986). It is only in modernity that differentiation took a top-down character. It reached, in other terms, society's social base.

Once a society is fully (i.e., both horizontally and vertically) differentiated, following Parsons, there is a problem of *integration*: of how to coordinate, to bring together the differentiated institutional subsystems so that increased "adaptive capacity" is achieved. For the father of modern sociological theory, modern societies tend to achieve a *balance* between institutional subsystems (economic, political, social, cultural) via quasi-automatic, systemic mechanisms (Parsons 1971: 27 and 1977). *Contra* Parsons, I think that under modern conditions, the integration of differentiated institutional spheres is not automatic, neither it is always *balancing* in the sense of always respecting the autonomy of each sphere. Often integration/coordination is achieved in a *levelling* manner, by a dominant institution (political or religious) undermining the autonomous logic of all other social spheres. In other terms social integration can take both monologic and polylogic forms (Mouzelis 2008: 49-54).

The differentiation of institutional spheres entails, of course, the differentiation of roles and a role player's identities. The multiplication of a subject's identities also requires by her/him integrative efforts. This condition generates intense anxiety which renders difficult the balanced integration of an individual's multiple and fluid identities. Therefore, integration can take both a balancing and levelling form. In the latter case, one of the subject's identities dominates all other identities undermining their relative autonomy and specific logic. This brings a rigid stability, reduces anxiety but inhibits the type of creativity that late modern conditions make possible. It may therefore lead to extreme forms of fanaticism (see Chapter II).

Widespread Individualization

It is more or less obvious that when social differentiation is not limited at the top, when it spreads downwards, people cannot anymore operate within an overall fixed traditional setting. A setting which is reducing individual choices and is not requiring coordination capacities as one moved from one institutional sphere to another. In modernity there is not only a multiplication of choices but the subject has to be able to coordinate the movement from one differentiated space to another on a more or less daily basis. This more complex situation requires new skills. It requires in the last analysis the capacity for the subject to actively "construct her/his own life, her/his own biography" (Giddens 1994).

I think that the massive inclusion of the population into the national centre, the top-down differentiation of institutional spheres and the large-scale individualization, *in their articulation*, constitute the uniqueness of modernity. This articulation, for technical and other reasons, could not and did not exist in any pre-modern social formation. Massive inclusion and top-down differentiation lead, on a horizontal level, to the relative separation of institutional spheres, while vertically, within each institutional sphere, a marked *homogenization* occurs; homogenization in the sense that certain features which in pre-modern social orders were confined among elites are spreading downwards[7]. For instance, a cultural feature like religious indifference or loss of faith is no longer limited to the sphere of intellectual virtuosi; it is adopted by a large section of the population[8]. And the same is true if one focuses on such traits as growing individuation, hybridity, relativism, ambiguity etc. Beck and Lau (2005), for instance, argue that whereas in early modernity ambiguity as a dispositional feature was limited to the elite level, in late modernity it spread downwards, it became a feature among the people in general.

To conclude this section, the uniqueness of modernity can be established less in cultural and more in socio-structural terms. It is only when socio-cultural features or dispositions are seen within the context of top-down institutional differentiation, extensive individualization and massive inclusion into the national centre that they acquire a unique status.

Present Day Globalised Modernity: Late Modern or Post-Modern?

There is an ongoing debate on whether the globalised modernity we are experiencing at present should be called late modern or post-modern. For the sake of expository convenience let us call "modernity A" the one primarily characterized by the rise of nationalism and the nation-state mainly in the 19th century; "modernity B" the one linked with the rapid globalization processes since the 70s. Those who stress *continuity* between modernity A and B call the former *early* modernity and the latter *late* modernity (see, for instance, Giddens 1990)[9].

---

[7] It is the spreading of socio-cultural traits downwards that Norbert Elias (1982 and 1991) has termed "basic democratization". The term is however confusing since by democratization we usually mean the adoption of representative institutions, voting rights etc. I think that "basic homogenization" is a better term.

[8] Charles Taylor (2007: 423) shows how in 19th century Europe we already have a proliferation of religious and non-religious positions from the educated elites to the less educated masses. The chasm between elites and non-elites diminishes as we see the emergence of similar religious and non-religious imaginaries between top and bottom, between countryside and town. For an extensive analysis of the pre-modern chasm between elite and popular religiosity in world religions, see Sharot 2001.

[9] For structural similarities between the transitions from pre-modernity to modernity and from modernity to late modernity, see Mouzelis 2008.

On the other hand, those who see a radical *discontinuity* between A and B prefer the term *post-modern* (see Bauman 1987 and 1992)[10]. It seems to me that the debate takes place at such a high level of abstraction that it becomes "unsettlable". One way out of this is to focus specifically on what happens to the unique social structural features of modernity as we move from modernity A to modernity B.

Global Mobilisation/Inclusion

As already argued in the first section, one major structural feature which is linked to the rise of the nation-state is the demise of segmental localism and the gradual mobilisation/inclusion of the whole population into the national "imagined community". To repeat, this process entailed the shift of material and symbolic resources from the periphery to the national centre, the concentration of the means of production, domination and influence in the hands of national elites and the unprecedented penetration of the periphery by state and national economic and cultural mechanisms. Needless to say, the mobilisation/inclusion process was not unilinear. It was marked by a continuous, long, drawn out struggle between local and national elites the former fighting against the centralizing strategies of the latter[11]. The eventual dominance of the centralizing state mechanisms was, of course, the result of not only intra- but also interstate struggles. In cases, for instance, in which we see a failure of the state to penetrate the periphery and reduce the autonomy of local potentates (e.g., Poland), the whole social formation collapses or is peripheralised (P. Anderson 1974).

Now if in *ideal typical terms*, we consider the type of globalized modernity that the dominance of neo-liberal capitalism brought about from the 70s onwards, one can identify similar processes as those which occurred in modernity A but on a global level this time. More precisely, if in modernity A we witness the loss of the local community's autonomy, with globalization we see the loss of autonomy of the nation state. Loss of autonomy does not mean of course the shrinking or peripheralisation of the state. On the contrary, the resources that the state extracts from society increase rather than decrease. What declines is the state's autonomy, its capacity to control within national boundaries processes like the movements of capital, migration flows, the spread of globally organised criminal networks etc[12].

Moreover, in the same way that in modernity A there is a shift of material and non-material resources from the local to the national level, a similar development occurs today from the national to the global level. We see a growing control of the global means of production, domination and persuasion/influence in the hands of

---

[10] For Bauman (1992) radical discontinuity is evident whether one looks at the cultural and socio-cultural features of present-day social formations, or at the ways in which social science discourses/narratives analyse or should analyse these formations.

[11] For concrete examples of this type of struggles during the period of nation-building, see Mouzelis 1986.

[12] On global flows and networks, see Castells 1996.

transnational elites[13]. A related isomorphic feature is the passage from the state penetration of the periphery to the penetration of global economic and political mechanisms to almost all national peripheries[14]. Finally, in the same way that the passage from the local/communal to the national level was not a linear, unopposed process, the same is true for the shift from the national to the global level. A variety of social forces (fundamentalist, nationalistic, ethno-populist) try either to reverse the globalization process or to change its neo-liberal character[15].

To sum up, if we take into consideration the isomorphic processes between modernity A and modernity B, I think that social structural *continuity* rather than discontinuity prevails. The logic of modernity is not interrupted, it continues as we move from the 20th to the 21st century.

Global Social Differentiation

A similar argument can be made if we look at the other major and unique social structural feature of modernity, that of top-down institutional differentiation. Here as well the "top" is not the national but the global centre as we witness the clear formation of distinct global institutional spheres, each portraying its own logic and historical trajectory. For globalization entails not only a global economy marked by the free movement of capital and the generation of unprecedented wealth, it also entails the formation of a global polity marked not, of course, by a world state but by a number of organizations (from the United Nations to the G20) which increasingly exercise to some degree global governance. And one can argue in a similar fashion as far as the formation of a global culture is concerned, a culture marked by a constellation of hybrid cultural complexes unified by a planet-wise consumerist ideology (Sklair 2002). Finally, globalization is leading to the formation of a global civil society within which transnational NGOs and new social movements focus on issues concerning global poverty, climate change, human rights violations etc.

Of course, some theorists have argued that in modernity B we see not only processes of growing social differentiation but also of *dedifferentiation*. For instance, the new information technologies make working from home possible. In such cases the differentiation between the domestic and the work sphere differentiation which occurred in early modernity with the passage from the putting out system to the factory[16] is reversed. On this point I would argue that

---

[13] See on this point Sklair 2002.
[14] This becomes obvious if one compares the 1860-1914 globalization to the present one. In the former case we also see an opening of world markets, the free movement of capital etc; but global market mechanisms were not able to penetrate the periphery of nation states open to the world economy. In present day globalization the penetration is striking. Many multinational corporations, due to the new communication technologies, have branches not only in all countries but also in the main urban centres of each country.
[15] For the development of this argument, see Habermas 1987. See, also, Mittelman 2000.
[16] For a description and explanation of the transition from the domestic to the factory system, see Smelser 1962.

processes of differentiation (as seen in the growing division of labour and extreme specialization in numerous fields) prevail over processes of de-differentiation[17]. Moreover one should also take into account that processes of dedifferentiation also occurred during the movement from pre-modernity to early modernity. As I have already argued, the decline of segmental localism and the process of massive inclusion into the national centre brought about a homogenisation of institutional spheres; it diminished the gap between elites and non-elites as various sociocultural trends (religious disbelief, individuation, reflexivity) spread downwards. This can be seen as a process of "vertical" dedifferentiation.

If finally, we look at specific institutional spheres, one can argue that in modernity B we see qualitative breaks, i.e., discontinuities rather than continuities. Particularly in the field of applied sciences, developments like the compression of time and space via the internet, or the generation of new risks[18] via genetic engineering constitute unprecedented phenomena. But against the discontinuity thesis one can argue that the above developments have their roots in modernity A. Moreover, in modernity A we also have unprecedented developments. For instance, nuclear physics and the construction of qualitatively new means of destruction (the atom bomb) created unprecedented risks of total annihilation.

Taking into account the above, it seems to me that continuity prevails over discontinuity. Particularly in social structural terms the logic of modernity B is an extension of modernity A's logic. Therefore, modernity B should be called *late* rather than *post*.

Modernity or Modernities?

It is common to identify modernity with the capitalist liberal democracies first developed in Western Europe[19]. In its mature form this type of modernity entails two major political features: a pluralistic party system (the liberal dimension) and extensive voting rights (the democratic dimension). Given the above, a usual critique of the modernity concept is that it is eurocentric that by modernization

---

[17] Ulrich Beck, in whose work the concept of differentiation plays a central role, has argued that in what he calls "modernity two" functional differentiation continues to develop. He makes however two further points which place him in the discontinuity rather than the continuity camp. First, he argues that as far as differentiation in modernity two is concerned, we see continuity on the level of basic "principles" and discontinuity on the level of institutions (Beck and Lau 2005: 532-533). Second, in modernity one differentiation generates problems that further differentiation controls/solves. In modernity two problems created by differentiation cannot any longer be solved by further differentiation (2005: 526ff).

[18] For an analysis of risks in early and late modernity, see Beck 1992. According to the German sociologist the difference between the former and the latter is that today, unlike the case in early modernity the "risk spiral" is no longer controllable. Therefore, in this case Beck adopts the discontinuity thesis.

[19] This is very obvious in the neo-evolutionist modernization theories which were based on the Parsonian tradition/modernity conceptualization. According to such theories third world "modernizing" countries, via the spread of western technology and institutions, will gradually resemble developed, democratically organized, capitalist western societies. See Parsons 1964 and Hoogvelt 1978.

one merely means westernization (Von Laue 1987). Even worse, the modernity/modernization discourse is used as an ideology at the service of western cultural and geopolitical imperialism (Douzinas 2000).

I think that the way in which I have conceptualized modernity in the previous sections allows one to use the concept in a non-Eurocentric manner[20]. It allows one to view the western liberal democratic order as one type of modernity which co-exists more or less antagonistically with other types. I have already pointed out that one basic feature of modernity is the decline of segmental localism and the large-scale mobilisation/inclusion of the population into the national centre. This "drawing-in" process however can take both *autonomous* and *heteronomous* forms. In the former case civil, political and socio-economic rights previously confined to the elite level spread gradually downwards (e.g., 19th century England). In the latter case people were brought into the expanding and centralizing mechanisms of the nation-state via conscription, taxation, national modes of surveillance etc. but were "left out" as far as the granting of political rights was concerned (e.g., Prussia in the 19th century).

The second feature of modernity, that of top-down differentiation of institutional spheres, is also useful as a means of constructing a typology of different modernities. One can thus distinguish different types of mechanisms which integrate the differentiated institutional spheres. There are *balanced* forms of integration, forms which respect the specific logic and relative autonomy of each sphere[21]. There are also *levelling* integrating mechanisms, in which case a dominant institution undermines the autonomy and "colonizes" [22] all other institutional spaces. The levelling type of integration does not necessarily lead to de-differentiation since we do not have a return to segmentalism. It leads to a *formal* rather than a *substantive* differentiation, since social roles (economic, religious etc.) retain their distinctiveness but lose, partly or entirely, their autonomous logic[23]. If one takes into account the above, than it is possible to construct in ideal typical but also theoretically congruent manner a typology of modernities.

---

[20] For an extensive development of this argument, see Mouzelis 2008.
[21] As far as social differentiation is concerned, this is exactly the type of modernity that Parsons (1977) refers to when he examines fully-developed western societies. According to the American theorist, in evolutionist terms, there is a systemic tendency towards balanced forms of integration in the modern world.
[22] The colonization term is used by Habermas to refer not only to authoritarian/totalitarian societies, but also to those having representative, democratic institutions. According to the German theorist, modern capitalist societies, democratic or not, have taken a wrong turn: political and economic institutions (what he calls the *system*) penetrate and dehumanize the institutions of the lifeworld (1987: 163ff). For a critique of this view, see McCarthy 1985 and Mouzelis 1991: 172-193.
[23] Another way of putting it is to argue that formal differentiation, in ideal typical terms, leads to a *monologic* type of institutional order, whereas substantive differentiation to a *polylogic* one. For the distinction between formal and substantive differentiation, see Mouzelis 2008: 150-151.

Liberal Democratic Modernity

In this case we have an autonomous/democratic "drawing-in" process and a more or less balanced integration of the differentiated institutional spheres. Needless to say a perfect balance between the values of productivity in the economic sphere, those of liberal democracy in the political, solidarity in the social and self-realization in the cultural, contra Parsons[24], was never achieved in Western Europe or anywhere else. However, during the so-called "golden period of social democracy" (1945-1975), the articulation of democratic/autonomous inclusion and relatively balanced forms of integration led to a capitalism with a "human face". This situation changed in the 70s and 80s. The rise of neo-liberal ideologies led to a situation where the market logic prevailed in several institutional spheres (education, politics, art etc); therefore integration, particularly in the Anglo-Saxon countries, took a less balancing, more levelling form.

An argument of those who criticize the modernity concept as eurocentric is that late developing countries are seen as modernizing via the diffusion of Western values, institutions and technologies therefore what we see is *westernization* rather than modernization as a process different from the western one. However, one can argue that to adopt institutions or technologies invented or fully developed in the West does not necessarily entail "servile" imitation. For instance as far as European "late-comers" are concerned (e.g. Germany) they have borrowed technologies first developed in England. This by no means led to the English domination or to the "anglicization" of continental Europe. In a certain way Germany's modernization, via a "leap frog" manner outpaced England in the 19th century[25]. If we do not consider German industrialization as anglicization why consider Japanese or Chinese industrialization/modernization as westernization?

A last point about the eurocentrism debate: the discourse on human rights and individual freedoms has also been criticized as eurocentric, as an ideological

---

[24] It is worth noting that for T. Parsons democracy, as it was fully institutionalized in the West, is an *evolutionary universal*: according to the American theorist, at present a society cannot move to higher levels of differentiation and adaptive capacity without democratizing, opening up its political system. It is by such an argument that he predicted, already in the 60s, the collapse of the Soviet Union (1964). I think that he was right as far as the demise of the USSR was concerned a *modern* system whose both the economic and the political sphere was closed. But cases like the Chinese one, in which a non-democratic political regime coexists with an open capitalist economic one are by no means doomed to extinction or peripheralisation. At present authoritarian capitalist modernization tends to portray higher levels of "adaptive capacity" than late developing countries with liberal democratic institutions. From this point of view democracy is not an evolutionary universal (Mouzelis 2008: 57ff). Of course, further economic development, via the creation of an important middle class may lead to an opening up of the political regimes of developmental authoritarianism. But this is a possibility, not a certainty. Therefore, the idea of the inevitability of the global prevalence of liberal democracy, as initially developed by Parsons (1964) and later by Fukuyama (1992) is quite dubious. Leaving aside *longue durée* predictions, in the short and medium term, under conditions of rapid globalization, both liberal democratic and authoritarian developmental modernities will coexist in an uneasy power equilibrium.
[25] On the competitive relations between England and Germany in the 19th century, see Hobsbawm 1968.

means for the consolidation of western global hegemony (Douzinas 2000). There is no doubt of course that often human rights and liberal democratic themes have been used for imperialistic, geopolitical reasons. It is also true that values related to human rights are not universal, "eternal" in the platonic sense. They are, for instance, less relevant or irrelevant in segmentally organised societies where social differentiation is low and the resulting individuation weak or non-existent (Mouzelis 2008: 164-175). However, the human rights discourse, although initially developed in the West, tends to become universally valued in all *post-traditional contexts*; i.e. in situations where top-down differentiation and high levels of individuation create subjects to whom democratic values appeal and this irrespective of whether such individuals live in democratic or authoritarian regimes. In other terms, human rights are not only appealing in democratic England or France, they are also appealing to those living in Chinese or Turkish urban centres. Human rights in other terms are not universally valid but they *tend to appeal transculturally* to subjects living in contexts marked by top-down differentiation and high individuation.

All the above suggest that if we define modernity by its unique social structural features (i.e., massive inclusion into the national centre, top-down differentiation and widespread individualization), it is possible to deal with modernization processes in a non-eurocentric manner. There is not one, there are several modernities one of which is the western. It is true of course that the two major social structural characteristics of modernity were first fully-developed in the West. But, as McNeil (1963 and 1995) has argued, the type of modernization that Western Europe experienced might have emerged at more or less the same time in other civilizations, civilizations which had equally favourable preconditions. If this is accepted, one can argue that the reason the breakthrough happened in Europe had less to do with unique elements (such as the protestant work ethic) and more with the *conjunctural* combination of elements that were not unique i.e., that could be found in other complex civilizations during the breakthrough period (e.g., China).

Authoritarian-Developmental Modernity

The most obvious and striking example here is the modernising trajectory of China. The mobilisation/inclusion process took momentum during the Maoist period and was accentuated with the spectacular capitalist development during the last three decades; a development which led from a quasi-totalitarian to an authoritarian/dictatorial capitalist regime within which the communist party reigns supreme. It is a regime which has opened up its economy but kept its political system closed. Its phenomenal capitalist growth is based on an export oriented opening to the world economy, the attraction of foreign capital and the political suppression of its labour force.

In terms of our definition of modernity we see in the Chinese case a process of state penetration and a quasi-heteronomous inclusion into the national centre; quasi-heteronomous in the sense that there is a clear separation between state and capital, the latter enjoying a considerable degree of autonomy. The same, of course, is not true about labour or about civil society groups religious, ethnic etc. We also witness a top-down differentiation, as the non-differentiated traditional communities, particularly in the coastal areas, decline. As to the integration of the differentiated institutional spheres this has a quasi-levelling character since the dominant political sphere (to a lesser extent than in the totalitarian cases) undermine the autonomy of all other non-economic spheres (educational, religious, kinship, ethnic etc.). As to future prospects, for some observers, Chinese modernization will follow the pattern of other south-eastern modernizing cases (e.g., S. Korea, Taiwan). In the latter an initial authoritarian/dictatorial phase of export-oriented capitalist development generated a new middle class which pressed for a modest opening of the political system. According to other analyses however, the control that the Chinese Communist Party exercises over both foreign and indigenous capitalist investors is such that the opening up process is not very probable at least not in the near future.

Finally we find an attenuated variant of authoritarian modernity in a number of "late-late"[26] developing countries. Here state penetration and massive inclusion into the centre also takes a quasi-heteronomous form since democratic institutions are minimally or superficially democratic. In such cases an anti-developmental state systematically subordinates the logic of all institutional spheres to the clientelistic and/or populistic logic of political domination (Mouzelis 1994).

Totalitarian Modernity

Authoritarian modernities can take totalitarian or quasi-totalitarian forms as in the Nazi or the Soviet type of modernizations. In such cases we have the decline of segmental localism, the large-scale mobilisation/inclusion into the centre but without the granting of civil and political rights to the population at large. We have in other terms an heteronomous type of inclusion. As to social differentiation, we see a marked levelling type of integration: the political sphere, particularly the party machine undermines the autonomy of all other institutional spheres[27].

In the Nazi case the levelling was not total. The economic, capitalist sphere, although state-regulated, did enjoy a certain degree of autonomy. On the other hand in the Soviet Union the levelling process was more accentuated. What I would like to stress here is that there is no reason to consider the soviet type of regime non-modern or transitory. It lasted for almost a century and it still survives in North Korea. Non-capitalist economic and political development may have, to

---

[26] The "late-late" term, which is used extensively in the development literature, aims at distinguishing the (compared to England) relatively late European industrializers (Germany and France) from those semi-peripheral societies which experienced large-scale industrialization a century or more later. See Hirschman 1970: ch. 3.
[27] For some students of the Soviet Union or Nazi Germany, the state was not totalitarian since it did not manage to reduce completely the autonomy of all institutional spheres. If, however, we take into account that in the context of this article the typology of modernities is based on an ideal typical analysis, I think that the term totalitarian is quite appropriate.

use Parsonian terminology, lesser adaptive capacity[28] but in terms of inclusion and top-down differentiation, it is certainly modern. The fact that such regimes have collapsed or are in the process of collapsing is not a good reason to consider them as non-modern. To put it differently, it makes no sense to call English or German industrialization modern and soviet industrialization non-modern or pre-modern[29].

---

[28] For the concept of adaptive capacity, see Parsons 1977. Parsons' idea that in modernity the movement towards higher levels of adaptive capacity presupposes the adoption of democratic institutions (see Parsons 1964), quite obviously does not apply in the case of China and of other Asian capitalist societies. In more general terms, Luhmann (1982) is right when he argues that greater differentiation does not necessarily lead to greater adaptive capacity.

[29] Giddens (1985), for instance, views capitalism as a constitutive component of modernity (together with industrialism and the centralized means of violence and surveillance). Therefore, non-capitalist industrializing societies are considered non-modern. Hall and Grieben also view capitalism as a necessary feature of modernity and argue that pre-1989 Eastern European societies are exceptions (1992: introduction). On the other hand there are theorists who view capitalism as a type of modern society. See Crook et al. 1992 and Wagner 1994.

Chapter 2

Modernity: Religious Trends

By conceptualising modernity in sociostructural rather than cultural terms, I will try (a) to show how modernity's sociostructural features are linked to religious developments particularly in the Anglo-Saxon world; (b) to examine critically the ongoing secularization debate in the social sciences. As I have pointed already, modernity can be seen as the type of social organization which became dominant in the west after the English industrial and the French revolutions. It entails three broad structural traits which render modern society *unique* unique in the sense that the above characteristics, in their combination, are not to be found in any pre-modern social formation. These characteristics are:

- the demise of segmental localism and the mobilisation/inclusion of a whole population into the national centre/nation state.

- the overall differentiation of institutional spheres.

- the spread of individualization from the elite to the non-elite level.

Massive Inclusion into the National Centre: The Process of Religious Rationalization

As mentioned in Chapter I, inclusion into the centre and the concentration of the means of economic, political and cultural production at the top meant that the pre-modern *dualism* between a traditional non differentiated periphery and a differentiated centre was attenuated. In the religious sphere the pre-modern dualism was between an elite and a folk, popular religiosity. The former was characterised by scripturalism, a focus on sacred texts, their "correct" interpretation and by an internal coherence/rationality of theological doctrine. Popular religiosity on the other hand was less "pure", since communal and religious traditions were inextricably linked together Christian religious beliefs coexisting with superstitions and magical or pagan ideas and practices. With modernization the above religious divide was attenuated as elements of the official doctrine spread "downwards"[1].

---

[1] For the chasm between elite and popular religiosity in several religious traditions, see Sharot 2001.

More specifically, if we focus on pre-industrial Christian Europe, in the rural areas a hybrid situation prevailed. Christian dogmas and rituals coming from above were coexisting with non-Christian ones, the latter emanating from communal/village pagan traditions and from beliefs in magical codes, spirits, demons etc. Gradually the latter beliefs and practices were marginalised and church organizations penetrated the rural periphery, exercising a more direct influence on both local clergy and laity. The attenuation of the chasm between official and popular religiosity meant a *homogenization* of the religious sphere proper. Given that homogenization processes had on the whole a top bottom direction, it did not necessarily lead to decreasing inequalities rather the opposite occurred. For the homogenizing process tend to enhance the control that religious elites have over the laity. If in modernity we see a concentration of the means of production, domination and violence at the national centre, the same can be said about the "means of religious influence or indoctrination". Elites at the centre are more capable of imposing religious "orthodoxy" to those at the periphery.

Growing homogenization tends to increase power inequalities between religious elites and non-elites; at the same time, it also increases *religious rationalization*. Following Max Weber, religious rationalization not only entails successful attempts at spreading the official doctrine downwards eliminating thus magical or foreign to that doctrine elements; it may also entail rendering the church's belief system (via for instance more flexible interpretation of sacred texts) more consistent internally or more compatible with scientific developments (Weber 1925: 538ff).

However, if religious rationalization entails the elimination of magical elements from the ecclesiastical space, one should stress that rationalizing tendencies in late modernity can go hand in hand with "derationalizing" ones. The latter tendencies may refer, for instance, to the type of hybridity which consists in combining church membership and attendance with beliefs and practices incompatible or foreign to the official dogma such as Buddhist meditation techniques, beliefs in reincarnation etc. Therefore the pre-modern, traditional hybridity entailing a mixture of Christian and superstitious/magical elements is replaced in globalised modernity by a post-modern hybridity entailing a mixture of elements derived from various religious traditions. It may also entail the revival of magic, this time in a detraditionalized social context.

At this point, it is necessary to examine briefly the distinction between religion and magic. The distinction is not of course clearcut, but in ideal typical terms it is possible to differentiate the magical from the religious logic. For Marcel Mauss (1972) for instance magical practices tend to be more secretive and esoteric. The magician, in order to maintain her/his secret knowledge does not perform publicly, s/he is usually not related to any organization; s/he is self-employed, basing her/his authority less on a bureaucratic/organizational position and more on charisma and on extraordinary occult powers. Weber on the other hand stresses more the fact that magic is less oriented to the worship or contemplation of the divine and more to its use for achieving specific results: "Whoever possesses the requisite charisma for employing the proper means is stronger even than the god, whom he can compel to do his will. In these cases, religious behaviour is not worship of the God but rather coercion of the God, and invocation is not prayers but rather the exercise of magical formulae" (1925: 422).

The analytic distinction between the magical and the religious, despite its fuzziness, is important to make here because the former via innumerable publications, the mass media and the internet, has ceased to characterise the activities of illiterate peasants or of a small number of initiates. As the shelves of major bookshops the world over testify, the global market for books on witchcraft, occultism, astrology and related themes is huge and growing in geometrical fashion. Perhaps nothing indicates better the global, late modern interest in the magical than the Harry Potter books which have been translated in more than a hundred languages and have sold millions of copies. Of course the interest in magicians, sorcerers and witches does not mean an active participation or exercise of magical/occult practices. But, at least indirectly, it clearly indicates a marked trend towards the "remagicalization" of the world. In the light of the above, one can argue that, on the one hand modernity's inclusionary processes have weakened the chasm between elite and popular religiosity, eliminating thus the magical/superstitious elements of the traditional, local communal culture this leading to *religious rationalization*. On the other hand however, particularly in the non-institutionalized religious space of late modernity the magical reappears and acquires global dimensions, strengthening thus *derationalization processes*.

A last point about modernity's inclusionary processes. The spreading of elite elements downwards does not only entail the trend towards religious rationalization. For if secularity (in the form of indifference to religion, agnosticism or atheism) was in pre-modern times limited among philosophers and a small fraction of the educated classes, with the advent of modernity secular orientations are also spreading downwards among people in all walks of life. This brings us to an examination of the secularization debate.

Top-Down Differentiation of Institutional Spheres: The Issue of Secularization

A) Moving to the second sociostructural feature of modernity, the decline of localism and the massive mobilisation/inclusion into the national centre was not merely a quantitative move from the small to the large. In systemic terms, the drawing in process took place in a context of rapid and thorough differentiation as institutional spheres (economic, political, social, religious, cultural) started portraying their own logic, their own reproductive technologies, their own historical trajectories.

Structural-functional differentiation is not, of course, unique to modernity. Complex pre-industrial social formations such as empires also portray a considerable degree of differentiation (Eisenstadt 1963). But as Marx (1859) and others have pointed out, in such societies this process was limited to the top. The differentiated parts or subsystems of the centre were superimposed on the non-differentiated, segmentally organised peripheries. This means that the degree of penetration of the centralized economic, political, and cultural apparatuses are both very weak and highly uneven (Mann 1986). It is only in modernity that differentiation took a top-down character. It reached, in other terms, society's social base (see Chapter I).

B) The above processes had an important impact in the religious sphere. Growing social differentiation meant that religion had a lesser direct impact on the other institutional spheres educational, recreational, professional, artistic etc. This *interinstitutional* secularization occurred gradually and had neither a linear nor a unidirectional character. For, on the one hand there was a weakening of the overall integrative role that the church was exercising in pre-modern times, but on the other hand, in late modernity there was a process of a new involvement of the church in the political or public sphere (i.e., a process of dedifferentiation), as the clearcut distinction between "God and Caesar" was often blurred. For instance, the critique of liberal protestant religious elites in the United Kingdom against neo-liberal, Thacherite social policies undermined the strict differentiation between the religious and the public sphere. And this is more so in the case of liberation theology and the dynamic political involvement of catholic priests in several Latin American countries. And equally striking, as an example of dedifferentiation between the religious and the political, is the growth of the evangelical right in the USA[2]. Finally, the ethno-religious features of orthodox churches in eastern and southern Europe (e.g., Poland and Greece) shows if not dedifferentiation, a patriotic/nationalist resistance to the differentiation between church and polity.

All the above cases of interinstitutional dedifferentiation however disprove the linear version of the secularization thesis but not the non-linear, "general evolution" one. At least as far as Christianity is concerned, the *overall* loss of direct control of the churches over other institutional spheres, as a general trend, is both dominant and *irreversible*. The crucial, society wide integrative role of religion, its deep intrusion in all social spheres that we see in most pre-modern situations has disappeared for good at least in the West[3].

C) If in *interinstitutional terms* (i.e., in terms of the relationship between the religious and society's other institutional spheres) secularization as a long-term process is evident, the same does not apply when we focus on developments within the religious sphere itself. Here the secularization thesis is much weaker. The strength and vitality of various denominations in the USA, the rapid growth

---

[2] These cases of the churches' political involvement indicate a reversal of the trend which characterised the early postwar period (see Martin 2011: 23-24).

[3] The situation is quite different in the Islamic world. Here not only the non-differentiation between polity and religion is fully legitised by the Qur'an, but also the partial secularization that occurred during the shah period in Iran was reversed by a revolution which led to a theocracy. Present day Iran is of course modern in the sense that the core sociostructural features of modernity are present. In fact, we see in the contemporary Iranian society the demise of segmental localism, state penetration of the periphery and massive inclusion into the national centre, as well as overall individualization. But the integration of the differentiated spheres is achieved in a levelling rather than balancing fashion; the religious logic penetrates and reduces the autonomy of most other institutional sphere (educational, recreational, professional etc.). Therefore, in the Iranian case we do not have *substantive* but *formal* differentiation or dedifferentiation (see Mouzelis 2008: 150-151).

of the so called new religious movements, the proliferation of religious informal groups or networks loosely linked to established churches and the phenomenal dynamism of Pentecostalism both in the first and third world (Martin 2005: 26-43) all the above indicate a weakening of *intra-institutional* secularization. They indicate clearly that intra-institutional secularity is not a constitutive element of late modernity. *Modern social structures are compatible with both secularity and non-secularity*. In other terms, further industrialization/modernization in the first and third world, contra Bryan Wilson (1966, 1982 and 2001), does not necessarily lead to secularization within the religious sphere. In many cases the opposite prevails. At present, the reaction to the logocentrism and to the faith in scientific and technological "progress" that the 18th century enlightenment culture propagated, render atheism and particularly the militant atheism of the R. Dawkins type rather ineffective.

Steve Bruce, in an attempt (2011) to defend the secularization thesis (both the inter- and intra-institutional one) considers religious liberalization as secularization. According to Bruce, once the medieval church was fragmented, there were steps towards secularity. This was true about the Reformation and even more so about the religious revival of the seventies. Given the latter's hostility to organizational authority and its focus on individual choice, the new religious phenomena are fragile, they are bound to decline and to lead to further secularization.

However, if secularization is defined in such an all-inclusive manner, one saves the theory but at the price of reducing it to obviousness. Against Bruce's thesis one can argue that the move from the non-fragmented, traditional medieval Catholicism to the Reformation is not a step towards secularity, but towards a different type of religiosity. And the same is true about the move, following Charles Taylor's typology (see below), from the denominational/ "mobilisation" to the "expressivist" postsecular model. That the latter, particularly when it refers to non-churched believers, is less institutionalised, more fragile, does not mean that it is bound to fizzle out, to lead to total religious indifference or atheism.

Steve Bruce referring to Parsons' theory of religious development, argues that "freedom from entanglements with secular power allowed churches to concentrate on their core task and thus become what Talcott Parsons called 'a more specialised agency', their removal from the centre of public life reduced their contact with, and relevance for, the general population" (2011: 35-36). Now it is true of course that in terms of the differentiation between the religious from the other social spheres (i.e., in interinstitutional terms) religion, with some exceptions, has been removed "from the centre of public life". But this does not entail, in intra-institutional terms, a weakening of faith. Bruce takes seriously into account only the part of Parsonian theory which stresses the differentiation between religion and the public sphere. But he does not take into account that for the American theorist differentiation entails both the relative shrinking of the church's influence in relation to other social spheres and a certain religious deepening among believers. To take two extreme cases: The automatic, taken for granted attitude of the traditional peasant towards the church is not more "religious" than that of today's non-churched believers. The beliefs of the latter may be more fragile, but one can argue that, at the same time, they are more "authentic" in the sense that they entail a continuous turning inwards, an internal process of exploration which is absent in the former case. Therefore "fragility" is not necessarily the last step before full secularization.

As far as future developments are concerned, I think that in addition to the rapid global growth of Evangelical and Pentecostal Christianity, non-churched religiosity given growing individualization (see below) has a great growth potential, particularly among the young. Bruce's idea that the young generation, through socialisation, adopt their parents' secular values (2011: 69-71) does not take into account intergenerational conflict, a phenomenon particularly marked from the counter-cultural sixties up to the present. After all the reaction to enlightenment's faith in instrumental reason is not limited to the restricted circles of postsecular theologians and philosophers; postsecularity is also spreading downwards. I believe that this reaction, as well as the turn to an ultra-individualistic form of religiosity is here to stay.

D) A different type of critique of the secularization thesis is developed by the distinguished British sociologist David Martin. In his more recent works (2005 and 2011), he has developed a general theory of secularization. He has argued, quite convincingly, against a linear view of the secularization process. Equally convincingly he claimed that the only secularising process which is in the long term irreversible is the one linked to social differentiation.

With this as a background, he has put forward the interesting idea that, from a macro-historical point of view, rather than growing secularization or desecularization, what we see in the west is a *constant dialectic* between the secular and the non-secular. Within the religious sphere there are periods of intense religious flourishing which at some point is weakening leading to secularising tendencies. In turn the latter tendencies are undermined by a new religious revival. Thus there is a tension between "spirit" and "nature", between a transforming Christian vision of peace and compassion and the realities of power and violence. As the spirit (divine grace) penetrates the "world", at some point the vision's initial élan is diminished and the religious thrust recoils[4]. As for the character of the recoil, it is affected by the cost that each religious drive entails: "Crucially I argue that instead of regarding secularization as once-for-all unilateral process, one might rather think in terms of successive christianizations followed or accompanied be recoils. Each christianization is a salient of faith driven into the secular from a different angle, each pays a characteristic cost which affects the character of the recoil, and each undergoes a partial collapse into some version of 'nature'" (2005: 3).

David Martin considers his secularization-desecularization dialectic as a general theory which applies at least in the Christian world, from the late antiquity up to the present. This broad scope however raises serious difficulties. When he

---

[4] The spirit-nature or the vision-power dialectic reminds one of Weber's charisma-routinization dialectic (Weber 1925: 246-254). The routinization or bureaucratization of charisma is analogous to the "naturalization" or institutionalization of the vision.

refers for instance to the early catholic christianization entailing the "conversion of monarchs (and so of peoples)" (2005: 3), he does not take seriously into account that secularity (in the forms of atheism, agnosticism, total indifference to religious matters etc.), during the first centuries of the church's history was limited to the elite level. Secularity in other terms was, during this early period, an exception. The bulk of the population was religious in a variety of ways, Christian, non-Christian or mixtures of both. As I have already argued, it is only with the dominance of modernity in the 19th century that the secular as well as the religious (in its non-pagan, elite form) spreads to the social base. In early Christianity as well as in the Middle Ages the major dynamic was less between the secular and the religious and more between different types of religiosity: between Christian and pagan religiosity, between eastern and western Christianity, between official versions of the Christian doctrine and a huge variety of "heresies" etc. Although David Martin does not specify when the move of the monarch type of catholic christianization recoils or what form the recoil takes, it certainly did not take the secular form since secularity, to repeat, was in pre-modernity restricted at the elite level.

In the light of the above I would argue that Martin's theory makes more sense if it is applied much later, in the period (from the 19th century onwards) when the three social structural features of western modernity were becoming dominant. It is during this period that massive inclusion into the national centre, top-down differentiation and widespread individualization created a relatively differentiated, autonomous religious sphere within which the chasm between official and popular religiosity receded this leading to the spread of elite religious elements downwards while at the same time secularity spread from intellectuals, philosophers and the educated classes to the popular strata. It is within this new "spreading downwards" context that it is useful to examine the dialectic between secularization and desecularization. One sees this dialectic, as Martin points out, in the various religious "awakenings" in the United States awakenings leading to religious expansion followed by "recoiling".

It should be stressed however that the recoiling of the Christian spirit may lead to "nature" and/or domination; but, it may also lead to non-Christian religious traditions and subcultures. If the former can be viewed from a "spirit-nature" or secularization-desecularization dialectic, the latter refers to a different type of dialectic dialectic between Christian and non-Christian beliefs, or between different types of religious hybridities. In late modernity the turning away from the Christian faith and the consequent developments of the new religious movements or of the New Age spiritualities cannot be dismissed as trivial and as bound to disappear. Given modernity's widespread individualization (see below), despite the lack of solid institutional supports and rituals, the new spirituality and the *à la carte* construction of one's religious voyage is here to stay even to grow. A general theory of secularization should explore the conditions under which the decline or recoiling of the Christian faith leads to secularity and those under which it leads to non-Christian or hybrid religious forms.

Another type of dialectic which is particularly important today is the liberal *versus* conservative one. As is well known, the counter culture of the sixties[5] and the new spiritualities which followed have led to a subjectivist, expressivist religiosity which stresses less attachment to sacred texts, dogmas and organizational authority and more to "heart work", direct experience of the divine and, more generally, to the existential dimension of religious life. The rapid growth of the latter type of religious subculture has created severe tensions within the established churches between those who accepted and tried to introduce the new, liberal spirituality into the ecclesiastical order, and those conservative forces which reacted to the liberalising tendencies of sections of the clergy and laity. A strong reaction to church liberalization occurred in the United States where the evangelical right tried to expand its message of "return to the fundamentals" a return to be achieved by media control and the creation of powerful lobbies in Congress (Ammerman 1994: 43ff)[6]. Furthermore, the liberal-conservative religious conflict entered more forcefully the public sphere as ethical problems such as in vitro fertilization, abortion, euthanasia etc. became issues of popular concern. This brings us to the third sociostructural feature of modernity, that of overall individualization.

Overall Individualization: The New Spiritualities

A) As Giddens has pointed out, in traditional social orders codes of "formulaic truth" delineate rigidly an individual's space of decision-making. From mundane decisions concerning marriage, family size and everyday conduct, to those concerning ultimate existential problems of life or death, tradition provides recipes for action that individuals adhere to as a matter of course. In early modernity, on the other hand, traditional certainties are replaced by "collectivist" ones. Progressivism (the Enlightenment faith in the unlimited perfectability of human beings and of social orders based on science and technical rationality), the bureaucracies of the nation-state imposing "internal pacification" and exercising all-pervasive surveillance, collective class organization, universal welfare providing all with a minimum of security against "external" and non-manufactured risks all these mechanisms operate in early modernity in a manner quite similar to tradition in pre-modern contexts. They provide social members with a meaning in life and with clear guidelines or rules that drastically reduce the social spaces where decisions have to be made.

---

[5] On the counter culture of the sixties and the reaction to it, see Tipton 1982.
[6] In the differentiated religious sphere, one can identify, on the one hand, an open, liberal inclusionary process which stresses a flexible, symbolic interpretation of the bible, gender equality, genuine respect of other religious traditions etc. On the other hand, there is an authoritarian, inclusionary mode which discourages choice and demands strict compliance to dogmas and ethical rules.

In late, globalised modernity, however, both traditional and collectivist certainties decline or disappear. Such basic developments as the globalization of financial markets and services, instant electronic communication and, more generally, the drastic "compression of time and space" have led to "detraditionalization". Via such processes as disembedment, increases in mediated experience, pluralization of the life-worlds, and the emergence of contingent knowledge, detraditionalization creates a situation where routines lose their meaningfulness and their unquestioned moral authority. It creates a situation where individuals can resort to neither traditional truths nor collectivist certainties when taking decisions in their everyday lives. Deprived of traditional or collectivist guidance, they must, in other words, deal with "empty spaces". From whether or not to marry and have children, to what life-style to adopt and what type of identity to form (even what type of physical make-up to aim for via dietary regimes, aesthetic surgery, etc.) in all these areas the individual has to be highly reflexive, and must construct "her/his own biography" (Giddens 1994).

One can argue of course that highly reflexive modes of existence can be found on the elite level in several pre-modern, complex societies. It is, however, only in late modernity that, given massive inclusion into the centre and top-down differentiation, subjects on the non-elite level are called, under conditions of detraditionalization, to create their own rules, to create "a life of their own" (Beck & Beck-Gernsheim 2003).

B) In the religious sphere now, the above bring us from Wilson's and Bruce's secularization thesis and Martin's secularization-desecularization dialectic to Charles Taylor's views on the secular age and beyond. The catholic philosopher's magisterial analysis (2007) is partly based on the construction of a threefold typology. The first ideal typical model, the *ancien regime* or *paleo-Durkheimian* one is not clearly differentiated from the traditional local community. Within it the faithful do not choose in the sense that they accept unquestionably the church's dogmas and ritual practices and are church members from birth to death. The second *neo-Durkheimian* or mobilisation model has its origins in the Reformation and refers to a situation where established churches adopt practices which focus less on dogma and strict rituals and more on a flexible, liberal framework. Particularly in the flourishing American denominations, the idea of choice becomes dominant, i.e., the idea that no church, no denomination has the monopoly of truth and that therefore the faithful have the right to explore and to choose. The third *expressivist* model, having its roots in 19th century romanticism, has developed in a spectacular manner among the youth from the seventies onwards. I will focus on the latter model since it is directly relevant to modernity's feature of widespread individualization.

Charles Taylor calls the complex of values underlying the above model *expressive individualism*. Expressive individualism reacts against dogmas and the authority of hierarchically organised religious elites. Religious truth cannot be found in sacramental mysteries, ex cathedra theological discourses or sacred texts. The authentic search for the divine is based on unmediated experience, on a turning inwards in an attempt to approach the divine existentially, in a manner resembling more the way of the mystic rather than that of the assiduous follower of rules and beliefs emanating from priestly authority.

Expressive individualism can be found both within the established churches and outside them. In the former case one sees a growing flexibility, a tolerance of diverging religious views[7] as well as a more general "liberalization" of beliefs and practices. As far as the space outside the well-established religious organizations, this is occupied by the so called new religious movements which may be Christian or may be oriented to other religious traditions (Glock & Bellah 1976, Robbins 1988). It is also occupied by fluid informal groups and networks which are usually loosely connected to more stable Christian denominations or congregations. Finally, within this extra-ecclesiastical space one finds "seekers" who are in a constant search, a continuous quest moving from one religious network or guru to another, often eclectically choosing elements from a variety of religious traditions both Christian and non-Christian[8]. Therefore in this particular case, in an attempt to achieve "authenticity" (Taylor 2002: 83), the subject constructs a religious path of her/his own; to paraphrase Giddens' terminology, s/he constructs her/his own "religious biography" (1994). It is here of course that the individualizing, expressivist features of modernity reach their zenith.

According to Taylor this type of ultra-subjectivistic, privatised religiosity can often lead to a trivialization of the religious life, to a situation where the picking and choosing from the global spiritual supermarket leads to an arid hybridity. On the other hand however he thinks that not all "New Age" type of developments can or should be dismissed in a facile manner. Some of these developments indicate young people's genuine search for a meaning in life that the globalised, consumerist, mediatised world cannot provide.

Assessing the present condition, the catholic philosopher posits two ways of leading a meaningful existence: "exclusive humanism" and "transcendental flourishing". Exclusive humanism can lead to an immanent, non-religious spirituality via the universalization of moral codes, the concern with nature, the struggles against world poverty etc. However, this type of humanism disconnects human beings from the cosmos and the mysteries of human existence. It leads to an "immanent flourishing", which is more limiting than the religious, transcendental spirituality of the Christian believer. Both however, according to Taylor (2007: 618ff), should be respected.

What I would like to add to the above is that between the secular, exclusive humanism and the transcendental flourishing there is a type of flourishing which is difficult to classify as secular or non-secular, a type of flourishing which is in

---

[7] This growing tolerance relates of course to the marked relativization of religious belief that globalization has brought about. Globalised modernity brings religious traditions closer to each other and this leads to hybrid forms of religiosity (Robertson 1989, Beyer 1994).

[8] For accounts of the "new spirituality", see Roof 2001, Fuller 2001, Herrick 2003, Heelas & Woodhead 2005, Heelas 2008, Wuthnow 1998, Douglas & Tipton 1983, Glock & Bellah 1976, Beckford & Luckman 1989, Robbins 1988, Carrete & King 2005.

the interface between secularity and non-secularity. This refers to the notion of the "indwelling God".

C) This is the view of those who believe that there is no God outside the human being, that the divine resides within us. God is entirely or exclusively indwelling. To put it differently, spiritual flourishing occurs when we discover and develop the internal to the subject "divine spark". Here as well there is infinity, but it is an "immanent infinity" an infinity referring to the depths and mysteries of the human soul. From this anthropocentric point of view to believe in an external deity leads to spiritual heteronomy, to an alienating type of religiosity. As Don Cupitt puts it, "unless religiousness is truly autonomous and subjective it is not religiously commendable. Piety cannot in any way be validated from the outside. Religious activity must be purely disinterested and therefore cannot depend upon any external facts such as an objective God or life after death. Furthermore, spiritual autonomy must not on any account be prejudiced, because there is no salvation without it. So, it is spiritual vulgarity and immaturity to demand an extra religious reality of God" (1980: 10)[9].

In the light of the above, if the religious entails a belief in an external to the individual divinity, belief in an exclusively "internal" God comes very near to secularity but it is not exactly secular since secularity entails unbelief, agnosticism or indifference in religious matters. If negative theology, in its western or eastern/orthodox version, considers that the divine, in its essence is external but unknowable, secular theology of the Don Cupitt or the J. Robinson (1973) type transforms external unknownability into the "internal" knownability of an exclusively indwelling deity. Needless to say the "indwelling God" theme is not limited in the restricted circle of secular theologians. As the secular and the non-secular, so the in-between theme has spread widely from the level of religious elites to the popular level. Heelas who called this trend *immanent spirituality* or *humanistic expressivism*, argues that a major feature of several New Age spiritualities is that God is not an external to the human being but a higher part of the self (Heelas & Woodhead 2005: 71ff, Heelas 2008: 55-58).

D) Another typical case situated between the secular and the non-secular is that of the so called "spiritual seeker". As Charles Taylor and many other observers have pointed out, expressive religiosity can take the form of a seeker's continuous spiritual quest, a seeker who rejects the dogmas, rituals and the bureaucratic authority of established churches and opts for an indivisualistic, continuous religious exploration. Such a spiritual exploration can be of two kinds. In the first case the seeker tries to explore the religious sphere in a proactive, *cataphatic* manner. S/he becomes familiar with the sacred texts and moral codes of various religions in an attempt to find elements which make sense to her/him,

---

[9] Continuing his argument, Cupitt affirms that "there can be for us nothing but the worlds that are constituted for us by our own language and activities. All meaning and truth and value are men-made and could not be otherwise" (1984: 20). The fact however that our language constitutes the reality we know cannot lead to the conclusion that there are no other realities. The reality of the mystic for instance is one that emerges when linguistic categories are suspended.

which meet her/his spiritual needs. In other terms here we have the case of the subject who in an activistic, decisionistic manner selects from the innumerable choices that the global religious space offers in order to construct her/his own unique, tailored made religious journey[10].

The other type of seeker, the one that interest us here, explores the spiritual space not in an energetic, voluntaristic, cataphatic manner but *apophatically*. Apophatic in Greek means negative. In eastern orthodox theology apophatism entails two basic elements. First that the divine, in its *essence* is totally transcendental and therefore unknowable, whereas in its *energies* it is approachable in a personal, direct, non-mediated manner. Second, the way to come near the divine energies is by getting rid of all passions, all calculations, all thoughts or even images. In this way the apophatically oriented subject achieves an "emptying out", s/he creates an internal void or rather becomes an "empty vessel" ready to receive God's energies or grace[11].

Whereas apophatism in the eastern orthodox tradition entails a belief in an external but unknowable (in its essence) God, there is a type of seeker who brackets so to speak the problem of God's existence. S/he tries, through contemplation and various meditation techniques to get rid of all thoughts, including beliefs in the existence of a divine force. Therefore in this case the seeker does not construct a "religious path of one's own"; rather s/he deconstructs habitual ways of acting and thinking, since the latter constitute obstacles to her/his self-realization. From this perspective the adoption of any type of belief system is anti-spiritual. It is an obstacle in the attempt to achieve an empty space within which how to live and what to do emerges spontaneously from within. In this way the "tyranny of choices" is overcome. What to do in any specific situation does not entail thinking, it rather entails not thinking (see on this point Chapter V).

Perhaps the spiritual leader who has developed most this type of faithless spirituality is J. Krishnamurti (1978 and 1985). For the Indian sage thinking and being are antithetical processes, the more one thinks the more one is getting away from the spiritual mode of being. Not only mundane thinking, ruminations or calculations but even believing in a transcendental reality or in an after life takes one away from genuine spirituality in the here and now. Belief of any kind is not only irrelevant but it also constitutes a serious obstacle to the spiritual quest. For spirituality is a "pathless way". It basically entails constantly observing what goes on inside the self in a wordless, conceptless, detached manner. When one comes near to this type of condition, the dualism between the observer and the observed disappears. What emerges is a limitless compassion *vis-à-vis* the self, the other and nature (for a further development of Krishnamurti's positions, particularly on

---

[10] This is the type of reflexivity that Giddens (1994) analyses when he refers to the process of reflexive modernization in post-traditional orders. See on this point Mouzelis 1999: 84-87. For those who "believe without belonging", see Davie 1994.

[11] Apophatic theology, which has common elements with the western negative theology, was closely but not entirely linked with hesychasm (hesichia meaning quietness), a spiritual movement that acquired importance in the late Byzantine period. Its major representative was St. Gregory Palamas (Meyendorff 1974).

ethics, see Chapter V). This type of "agnostic" spirituality which comes very near Zen Buddhism cannot be called religious since it does not entail a belief in a transcendental or external to the subject divine reality. On the other hand it is not covered by Taylor's exclusive humanism. As with the "indwelling God" it lies in the interstice between the secular and the non-secular.

Finally it should be stressed that the distinction between cataphatic and apophatic spirituality is an ideal type one. In actual situations, both types of orientation contain cataphatic and apophatic elements. According to the type of search, however, one of the two is dominant.

Conclusion

I have tried to examine the linkages between late modern religious developments and the three sociostructural features of modernity: the massive inclusion into the centre, the top-down social differentiation and widespread individualization.

> i. As far as modernity's *inclusionary processes* are concerned, these lead to both secularization and desecularization. They also allow for both religious rationalization and derationalization. What is common to all four processes and what are constitutive elements of modernity, is the massive mobilisation/inclusion into the centre, which, in the religious sphere, led to the attenuation of the dualism between religious centre and religious periphery. This meant that not only elements of the official religiosity "spread downwards", but also that secularity as well has spread to the population at large. From this point of view, a central task of the sociology of religion is to examine how the four processes (secularization, desecularization, rationalization and derationalization) are dialectically linked to each other.
>
> ii. In terms of modernity's *social differentiation processes*, in the Christian west inter-institutional secularization (given modernity's top-down differentiation) is quite irreversible. The separation between church and state is not of course watertight. Religious elites enter the public sphere in their attempt to influence social policies. There are also attempts of more direct interventions into the political sphere by the evangelical right in the United States, by radical priests in Latin America and by other religious activists. But despite the above, religion has ceased irreversibly to be an overall regulator of social life. On the other hand, in intra-institutional terms, i.e., within the differentiated religious sphere proper, one sees in late modernity a process of desecularization or religious revival. Particularly in the Anglo-Saxon world, the values underlying C. Taylor's expressivist model have, in varying degrees, penetrated most

non fundamentalist established churches. The latter, in an attempt to "move with the times", have become more liberal both in theological and political terms. Theologically there is less emphasis on the dogmatic dimension (i.e., the search for the "correct" belief system) and more on the expressive and existential dimension of religiosity. Politically the orientations of the so called "progressive milieu" (concern for world poverty, inequalities, environmental deterioration, focus on gay rights and women's empowerment) are appealing to spiritually oriented people inside and outside the established churches[12]. This liberal wave has of course generated a variety of reactions. Conservatives try to go "against the times" opposing the "sexual revolution", gay and women priests, women's right to abortion etc.

iii. Moving to *widespread individualization*, the third major sociostructural feature of modernity, as far as religiosity is concerned, it enhances the non-institutionalised, extra-ecclesiastical space of the new religious movements or cults and the informal groups and religious networks whether the latter are linked to established churches or not. It also leads to the multiplication of individual "seekers" who, when cataphatically oriented, in a highly selective manner try to construct a religious "path of their own". When apophatically oriented, they are less interested in the variety of belief systems that the global spiritual situation offers and more to meditative practices (see Appendix I and II). The latter are either used for therapeutic purposes or, less superficially, for the creation of an internal space, a void which is a precondition for the spontaneous emergence of a spiritual mode of relating to the self, the other and the divine. Although non-churched spirituality has not replaced established religiosity, there is no doubt that the so called "cultic" or "holistic" or "progressive" milieu grows very fast indeed (Heelas 2008). As to Pentecostalism, the other rapidly ascending global religious force, it also has elective affinities with widespread individualization both in terms of its marked expressivity and in terms of its similarities with the protestant ethic, with its emphasis, particularly in the Third World, on hard work, strict moral standards and individual economic success.

---

[12] On the "progressive milieu" notion, see Lynch 2007.

I close by stressing once more that the three sociostructural features of modernity allow both secular and non-secular modes of existence. Given this, the relation between the two will be shaped in the future not only by structural but also by a variety of conjunctural developments economic or ecological crises, scientific discoveries, the future of Islamic fundamentalism etc. From this point of view neither the idea of a long-term secularization within the religious sphere, nor the idea of a secularization-desecularization dialectic help us to foresee the future linkages between the secular and the non-secular.

As far as modernity is concerned, what is certain is that given the demise of segmental localism, the massive inclusion into the centre, top-down differentiation and overall individualization, *choice* is a key element for understanding the present and future religious landscape. In matters religious, choice ceases to be the privilege or "burden" of the few, it spreads downwards. In other terms, it is not only religious elites, intellectuals or philosophers who ponder the meaning of life and the pros and cons of a secular or non-secular mode of existence. Religious affiliation ceases to be taken for granted; it is an issue which concerns people in all social strata. After all, in existential and religious matters, generalised choice, real or imagined, is what modernity is all about.

Chapter 3

Modernity: The Fundamentalist Dimension

The basic argument in this chapter is that fundamentalism is modern not only or primarily in terms of the material and organizational technologies that it uses. It is also modern in terms of its basic sociostructural features, features which have an elective affinity with the unique characteristics of modernity. Choosing Islamic fundamentalism as an example, I will also try to see how the sociostructural level of the phenomenon relates, not only to the cultural but also to the psychodynamic/psychoanalytic level.

On the Specifity of the Fundamentalist Phenomenon

I think that what distinguishes fundamentalism from pre-modern authoritarian religious movements or regimes are not so much the cultural/ideological features which are usually referred to in order to establish its features; such as the attempt to return to an idealized "golden" past, the literal interpretation of sacred texts, the creation and demonization of an external enemy which enhances the religious community, the distinction between the believers' pure way of life and the unbelievers' "contaminated" one etc [1]. Although such attributes characterize fundamentalism, they are not unique to it. Most of them are to be found in pre-modern religious authoritarianisms. Therefore, they do not establish its *specifity*. What makes fundamentalism quintenssially modern are its sociostructural features.

If, for example, we consider fundamentalism's authoritarian and often violent orientations (and I refer here to both physical and symbolic violence), it differs from religious oppression in a pre-modern, segmentally organized setting. In the latter case, low individuation means that traditional subjects experience religious discipline and restrictive rules in a qualitatively different way than in a modern social formation whose social structure is characterized by top-down differentiation and widespread individualization. To be more specific, it is one thing imposing the *sharia* in a traditional, non-differentiated community and quite different one imposing its rules on modern, highly individualized citizens who have greater need for autonomy and self-realization.

---

[1] For an exploration of such features, see Marty and Appleby 1994.

Fundamentalism: The Cultural Dimension

In cultural terms, religious fundamentalism is a reaction to modernism or rather to certain of its aspects; such as widespread secularization, religious relativism, libertarian sexual norms, the legitimation of homosexuality, feminism etc. This reaction is linked to a project aiming at a "return to fundamentals". In Islamic fundamentalism for instance, the focus is on a return to a past fraternal community (the *Ummah*), the strict observation of the sharia, the opposition to western cultural and geopolitical imperialism etc. Given the great variety of Islamic traditions, one can always find features which differ from one tradition to another[2]. For instance, in the shia tradition the emphasis is less on an idealized past and more to a future golden age when the hidden 12th *Imam* will appear again (Sachedina 1994: 410). Therefore, in this case we have a messianic redemption similar to Christ's second coming.

In all cases the return to a past or future golden age is highly selective (Eisenstandt 1999). Only certain cultural features of the tradition are selected in order to mobilize believers against a demonized foe who is responsible for all social ills. In this chapter I will use the Iranian case in order to examine the modern feature of religious fundamentalism. For instance, Khomeini appropriated and radicalized certain features of the original shia Islam (which was quietistic) in order to mobilize the believers against the Pahlavi regime. More generally, he "modernised" certain aspects of the religious tradition in order to make them compatible with the nation state. Another point worth mentioning is that Islamic fundamentalism is exclusivist in the sense that other religious faiths are not tolerated (e.g., jihadists aim at the islamisation of the world by more or less violent means). On the other hand, it is "inclusionist" in the sense that religion should penetrate/dominate all non-religious institutional spheres from education and recreation to politics and science. The ultimate end, as in totalitarian regimes[3], is the total transformation of the societal and personality systems.

There is also the dogma of the Koran's inerrancy which characterizes Christian fundamentalism as well. But careful selection of a sacred text's features which are useful for popular mobilisation distinguishes strict scriptural literalism from the Islamic fundamentalist interpretation of sacred texts. The contradiction between selectivity and inerrancy is usually solved by the distinction between more and less fundamental aspects of the Koran. There is also the notion of "dynamic interpretation"; given that Islam entails political struggle, one needs to interpret the fundamental koranic principles in the light of the ongoing war against infidels. For Sayyid Qutb, for instance, an activist interpretation of the Koran is necessary if people were to understand its true meaning[4].

---

[2] For differences between various fundamentalist traditions, see Bruce 1988.
[3] For certain scholars totalitarian regimes, as communism, are considered as fundamentalist in the secular/political rather than religious sense (Eisenstandt 1999). In this text fundamentalism refers exclusively to the religious dimension.
[4] See on this Calvert 2010, Sivan 1985 and Qutb 2000.

Fundamentalism: The Sociostructural Dimension

When conceptualised in *sociostructural* rather than cultural terms, modernity refers to the type of social organization which became dominant in the West after the Industrial Revolution in England and the revolution of 1789 in France. As already mentioned in Chapter I, it entails three basic features, which distinguishes it from all pre-modern social formations:

- The decline of segmental localism and the inclusion of the population into the national centre.

- The top-down differentiation of institutional spheres.

- Widespread individualization.

Inclusion into the National Centre

In ideal typical terms the decline of segmental localism meant the transformation of the traditional non differentiated local community into a less self-contained social whole open to the direct influence of broader social forces. It meant in other terms the inclusion of the whole population into the "imagined community" (Anderson 1991) of the nation state, into its wider economic, political and cultural arenas. This *inclusionary* process led to the transfer of material and symbolic resources from the periphery to the national centre. From an actors' perspective, it led to the concentration of not only the means of production, but also the means of domination/violence as well as the means of cultural influence into the hands of national rather than local/regional elites. It is via such mobilising, "bringing-in" processes that the modern state apparatus penetrated the periphery in a manner which was unthinkable in all pre-modern social formations, however despotic.

As mentioned in Chapter I, deep state penetration and the inclusionary process can take both *autonomous* and *heteronomous* forms. In the former case civic, political, socioeconomic and cultural rights spread gradually "downwards", this resulting into a strong civil society which operated as a buffer to state authoritarianism. In the heteronomous case people were brought into the centralized administrative, military and cultural mechanisms of the nation state but without the granting of rights[5]. On the basis of the above definition, one can view a fundamentalist regime as a form of *heteronomous inclusion* into the national, politico-religious centre. As to a fundamentalist movement, one can view it in a similar manner: as an attempt at imposing a set of "fundamental" religious principles[6].

---

[5] For the distinction between autonomous and heteronomous inclusionary processes, see Mouzelis 2008: 145-163.
[6] Traditional Islamic movements like the Wahabite which aimed at the islamisation of Arab society are called proto-fundamentalist by Eisenstandt (1999: 33-35).

Taking as an example the Iranian theocratic regime we can easily identify processes drawing believers into the national centre. This entails a shift of material and symbolic resources from the periphery to the centre; or to put it in *actors' terms*, it entails the concentration of the "means of salvation" from local to national religious elites. Moreover, from a macro-historical perspective, in pre-modern Iran, as in most traditional societies, one observes a marked divide between popular/folk religiosity at the periphery and "high Islam" at the centre. The former was closely linked to the local culture of the traditional community. It was characterized by illiteracy, the prevalence of oral traditions, beliefs in local saints as intermediaries between believers and God, superstitious/magical orientations etc. On the other hand high Islam was based on sacred texts, disconnected from localist traditions and "prejudices", as well as on religious specialists who codified and interpreted such texts[7]. The above divide was attenuated as administrative and material technologies of the national, politico-religious elites penetrated the periphery.

In the Iranian case, during the pre-Khomeini period, the shah's attempt at rapid but misdirected[8] modernisation (both in the agricultural and industrial sectors) led to rapid urbanization (Bharier 1971, Graham 1979) and the subsequent weakening of the traditional, non-differentiated, village community (Sachedina 1994: 418)[9]. These processes created a large underclass of urban[10], deracinated, peripheralised poor who were easily mobilised by anti-shah forces. Therefore, both during the pre-Khomeini and Khomeini period, we witness clearly modernity's process of mobilisation and inclusion into the broader political, religious and cultural arenas of the nation-state. This inclusionary process was heteronomous rather than autonomous in the sense that people were "brought-in" without the granting of political rights. Indeed at present the Iranian fundamentalist regime is sustained by such bodies as "the Guardians of the revolution", as well as by militias, the most important of which is the paramilitary, ideologically driven *Basij* organization. The latter played a key role in controlling dissidents and in systematically suppressing with more or less violent means[11] any opposition to the regime. At present, the Basij organization is engaged in such activities as internal security, law enforcement, organizing religious ceremonies, suppressing dissident gatherings, moral policing etc. It has branches in most towns and peripheral areas and is often linked to local mosques. It is by this type of mechanisms that the Iranian people are mobilised and brought into the politico-religious centre (Bakhash 1984, Bernard & Zalmay 1984, Arjomand 1988).

We have of course similar processes in several islamic countries (e.g., Egypt, Tunisia, Algeria etc.) which, after a period of nationalist socialist regimes were

---

[7] For the chasm between popular and high Islam, see Gellner 1969 and 1981. See also Sharot 2001: 3-19 and 202-210.
[8] For the mismanagement of the Iranian oil boom, see Graham 1979: 32-52 and 77-130.
[9] For the process of urbanization and its social impact, see Bharier 1971 and Graham 1979.
[10] One of the factors which explain why a Khomeini type revolution did not occur in Iraq has to do with the relative resilience of the traditional village community (Sachedina 1994: 438ff).
[11] Violent means included arbitrary arrests, executions and property confiscations (Bakhash 1984: 155).

followed by conservative autocracies. In the latter cases fundamentalist parties constituted the main quasi-legal organized opposition [12]. It is not therefore surprising that fundamentalist organizations like the Muslim Brotherhood played a crucial role in the Arab Spring movements (Rubin 2010). Needless to say, with rapid globalization the inclusionary process expands from the nation state to the so called "global village" level as people are brought into the global centre via deterritorialized networks, networks which recruit and bring into the transnational sphere believers ready to fight against western infidels.

Top-Down Differentiation

Moving from an actors' to a more systemic perspective, the second unique feature of modernity is the differentiation of national society into analytically distinct institutional spheres, each one, at least potentially, portraying its own values, logic and historical trajectory. It is true, of course, that pre-modern, complex social formations were also differentiated along economic, political and cultural lines. But in such cases, as already mentioned, the differentiation process was limited at the top. The societal base was typically organized along non differentiated segmental lines.

Levelling integration characterizes the fundamentalist case. Fundamentalist regimes oppose secularization and, in the case of Islam, aim at the "islamisation" of the whole society. For instance, in the Iranian case Khomeini's *cultural revolution* islamised the universities by the dismissal of thousands of teachers. The same was true in the armed forces; officers considered "westernised" were dismissed (Arjomand 1988). In the case of fundamentalist movements trying to take over the state, overall islamisation is one of their main objectives. For instance radical politico-religious movements, both in the Middle East and in Africa, want to impose the *sharia* and, more generally, the overall traditional religious logic in all social spheres. To the extent that this is achieved, we do not have institutional and role *dedifferentiation* in the sense that there is no return to segmental forms of social organization. The separation of roles remains, but roles lose their autonomous logic. It is important therefore, in order to avoid theoretical confusion, to replace the usual distinction between differentiation/dedifferentiation by the threefold one proposed here: *non differentiation* (segmental organization), *formal differentiation* (levelling integration of roles, identities/institutions) and *substantive differentiation* (balancing integration). Given that levelling, monologic integration is imposed on highly individualized subjects (i.e., subjects with marked self-realization needs), its repressive impact is qualitatively different from that experienced in pre-modern social formations. This brings us to an examination of the third unique feature of modernity, that of widespread individualization.

---

[12] See on this point Halliday 1994.

Widespread Individualization

The third sociostructural feature of modernity refers to the growth of reflexivity and the overall enhancement of individualization. As already mentioned, in modernity one has to create "a life of one's own"[13]. One can argue of course that individualization that modernity entails can be found in pre-modern situations, particularly among cultural elites. What is unique in late modernity however is that the type of reflexivity that detraditionalization entails spreads from the elite to the non-elite level. Individualization is not any more limited to philosophers and artists; it is to be found among people in all walks of life (see Chapter I).

It could be argued of course that the fundamentalist's monologic orientations, her/his fanaticism can be found in pre-modern contexts. However traditional fanaticism is qualitatively different from the fundamentalist's zealotism encountered in late modernity. The difference relates to the top-down differentiation and widespread individualization of the late modern era. These sociostructural features entail the necessity of replacing the already given, facilitating traditional framework by a "self-made" one; creating thus a fanaticism related to *the specific anxiety that late modern conditions produce*. In simpler terms the fanaticism of a religiously oriented traditional peasant is different from that of a late modern deracinated, highly individuated, urban unemployed believer.

Another specific fundamentalist characteristic which is related to modernity's unique sociostructural features is the vision of an overall, total transformation of society and personality. Such a grandiose vision could be imagined by pre-modern utopias but could not be seriously attempted in a traditional social formation characterized by a chasm between social differentiation at the top and non-differentiation at the social base. Segmental organization renders very difficult the type of mobilisation that overall, societal transformation entails. The idea of an overall, total societal transformation, as far as the possibility of its realization is concerned, is specifically modern. To the extent that modernity undermines traditional localisms (economic, political, cultural) and brings people into the national centre, the notion of overall total change of society and the subject emerges both as project and as realistic possibility. Maududi, a famous scholar whose thought had a great influence on the Muslim Brotherhood in the Middle east, insists on the necessity of total transformation of a believer's way of life: "A person cannot be a true Muslim if he fulfils Islamic obligations in his personal life but neglects Islamic teachings in his political and economic behaviour"[14].

---

[13] For the concept of individualization, see Beck and Beck-Gernsheim 2003. See also Giddens 1994.
[14] Quoted in Ahmad 1975: 487.

Fundamentalism: The Psychodynamic Dimension

Moving finally to a more psychodynamic/psychoanalytic dimension, one should raise the question of the type of subject (psychologically speaking) which, under favourable conditions, opts for a fundamentalist mode of existence. As far as our example of Islamic fundamentalism is concerned, by favourable conditions I mean well known socioeconomic and politico-religious features such as: large scale unemployment, urban poverty, peripheralisation of the educated middle-class youth, existence of religious schools which are against globalization and a modernist culture, aggressive post-colonial nationalism etc. To put it differently, given "fundamentalogenic"/sociostructural pressures as the ones mentioned above, what type of subject is likely to yield to such pressures? Why certain subjects react in a "fundamentalist" manner whereas others do not? Among major psychoanalytic approaches those of Freud, Melanie Klein and Jacques Lacan have been used by more recent psychoanalytically oriented theorists in order to explain the conscious and unconscious processes which lead a subject to the acceptance of radical/extremist fundamentalist orientations and practices.

The Freudian Perspective

Concerning the Freudian perspective for instance, Ruth Stein (2010) starts with Freud's theory of the primaeval horde and its revolt against a domineering father. The murder of the father by his rebellious sons entails both liberation and remorse these two elements leading to the creation of civilization. Ruth Stein reverses the Freudian narrative. In the case of the jidahist type of fundamentalism, the son identifies with the father and turns his back to the mother. He wants to please the father in a total, unconditional manner. According to Stein an extreme interpretation of the jihad notion is that an infidel has three options: to be islamised, to be subjugated economically and politically, or to be killed. Since this is Allah's will, the jihadist, by killing infidels follows a divine order. Moreover, in the case of the suicide bomber, by killing himself/herself and becoming a martyr, s/he shows in the most concrete way her/his unconditional love for the father/God. In psychoanalytic terms this means *regressive* identification with the father leading, in its extreme form, to total self-sacrifice. For the jidahist this is a passage from the anxieties that late modernity generates to a close reunion with the father/God. It is also a straightforward response to the humiliation and suffering that western colonialism and post-colonialism/neo-imperialism has inflicted and continues to inflict on the Islamic people.

According to Stein, it is not objective conditions such as abject poverty, social peripheralisation, extreme forms of exploitation etc. which lead to radical/jihadist fundamentalism. It is rather *the inner logic* of an extremist ideology which generates psychodynamic mechanisms leading the subject to resolve the oedipal complex in a regressive manner, in a manner which leads, not to the killing of the father, but rather to killing for the "love of the father"[15].

Stein's analysis is a clear example of a tendency in psychoanalytically oriented theories to explain fundamentalism (as well as similar phenomena such as racism, chauvinistic nationalism, anti-Semitism etc.) by focusing almost exclusively on psychodynamic processes; ignoring "objective" conditions, or at best, considering them as given. There is therefore no serious attempt to link in a *theoretically congruent manner* the psychodynamic with the social. This leads to reductionism, to a methodologically "jumping of levels", to the absorption of the social by the psychoanalytic. It is not therefore surprising that the author of *For the Love of the Father* argues that sociostructural, objective conditions such as poverty and social peripheralisation, contrary to the theories of Fanon and Said, cannot explain radical fundamentalism, since all over the world there are situations where extreme poverty and peripheralisation do not lead to the emergence of fundamentalism in general and of jihadism in particular. This will not do, if sociostructural conditions cannot in themselves explain radical fundamentalism, neither the logic of the jihadist discourse and its relation to the way the subject handles the oedipal situation can provide a satisfying explanation.

The way to avoid reductive explanations is to articulate in a non-*ad hoc* manner psychoanalytic processes with the unique sociostructural features of late modernity. For instance, the spread of fundamentalism is difficult in situations where extremely poor people are segmentally organised. Even in an Islamic country where the fundamentalist narrative prevails in urban centres, the still rural, traditional communities are more or less immune to "fundamentalogenic pressures". Fundamentalism, as already mentioned, entails massive mobilisation and inclusion into the broader national arenas of the nation sate. It is such processes which undermine segmental localism and shift orientations from the periphery to the national centre. When these processes have not yet penetrated the segmentally organised, non-differentiated social base, fundamentalism cannot take roots.

To take Iran as an example, before the shah's "white revolution", which entailed rapid economic development, radical fundamentalism existed as an ideology but did not have a serious impact on the rural population. It was the shah's grandiose plans for overall rapid modernisation of Iranian society that created conditions which undermined the non-differentiated traditional community and made possible the penetration of the state into the periphery. It is such conditions which led to the mobilisation against the shah's regime that Khomeini and his followers achieved in the 70s (Bharier 1971, Graham 1979). If all the above sociostructural conditions are bracketed or are completely ignored, a psychoanalytic explanation "hangs in the air" so to speak. It cannot explain why the fundamentalist logic takes root under certain conditions and has no serious impact in other social spaces. To put it in a more general way, since

---

[15] This basic argument is fully developed in Stein's (2010) introduction.

fundamentalism is a specifically modern phenomenon, you cannot explain it without taking seriously into account modernity's unique features to repeat, massive mobilisation and inclusion into the national centre, top-down differentiation and broad individualization.

The Kleinian Perspective

Moving from Freud to Melanie Klein (1946), her theory of the processes which lead to *splitting and projection* is also used in order to explain extreme nationalism, racism and other radical ideologies entailing similar to fundamentalism features. According to the Kleinian perspective, in her/his early development (the schizoid-paranoid phase), the infant experiences internalised objects, particularly the maternal breast as being good and bad. The aggressive part of the primitive ego is projected to the "bad" breast, whereas the benign ego is projected to the "good" one. This splitting is considerably attenuated in a subsequent phase (the depressive phase) as the subject starts feeling both her/his ego and the other as integrated and as possessing both good and bad objects. When this integration is not achieved, the splitting between good and bad elements is accentuated and the latter are projected to the other who is imagined as an enemy, as a demonised other[16].

In the Kleinian case as well, explanation of racism or fundamentalism as *collective phenomena* by mere reference to psychodynamic processes is not enough. To move in a non-reductive manner from the psychodynamic to the sociostructural, one should try to deal with the following basic issue: Objective sociostructural conditions such as poverty, religious ideologies and organizations, western cultural imperialism etc. have to be taken into account in order to explain why splitting and projection processes are oriented to western "infidels" rather than to other groups (e.g., tribal enemies). Given this, one has to show how psychodynamic processes articulate with *specific* "objective" sociostructural conditions. For instance, is urban poverty or anti-modernism which is the more important dimension? In other terms, it is not enough to produce a long list of plausible, relevant factors. One has to see which is the most relevant, how such factor relates with another and how the overall configuration of elements *articulates* with psychodynamic processes. This, of course, requires *contextualisation*[17]. When this exacting task is not done, when social conditions, if

---

[16] Moreover, the other is not only demonised but, through a process of *projective identification* (Clarke & Bird 1999), starts acquiring the features projected upon her/him. In the case of racism, the dominant subject considers the dominated other as dangerous and as inferior possessing thus the negative characteristics that the former cannot see and cannot bear within himself/herself (Elliot 1996, Wolfenstein 1997, Bracher 1997). In the case of fundamentalism, we have a double demonization. The Islamic fundamentalist demonizes the western other and the latter demonizes Muslims in general.

[17] Contextualisation is also necessary if one takes into account that subjects may adopt fundamentalist ideas and practices without portraying psychodynamic pathologies of the type that psychoanalysis spells out. In such cases one should raise the question: under what conditions psychoanalytically oriented explanations are relevant and under which they are less so?

mentioned at all, take the form of a "list" of disconnected factors, then reductionism cannot be avoided.

The Lacanian Perspective

Another important approach to the issue of violence, fundamentalist or not, focuses on the notion of the Lacanian *jouissance*. The infant's entrance into the sphere of language and the symbolic leads to the irreversible loss of the type of full jouissance that s/he enjoyed before the imposition of the "law of the father". The latter creates, via the "symbolic castration" the division between the conscious and the unconscious, alienation from the self and the other and a lack which can never be permanently sutured (Lacan 1977). From the above perspective, under objective conditions favouring fundamentalist tendencies, the subject may attempt to recapture the lost full jouissance of the pre-symbolic period by striving for a return to an idealised past, to a traditional community (e.g., the Islamic *Ummah*) within which perfect harmony, fraternal solidarity and ethical purity prevailed. According to fundamentalist ideology, it is the western subject, the imperialist other who has destroyed the idealised, traditional community. S/he has stolen from the believer's full jouissance. A way therefore to recapture it is via massive anti-imperialist, anti-western mobilisation, it is by resisting and attacking the western "satan".

Another way of expressing in Lacanian terms something similar is to use the notions of identity and identification[18]. The subject tries to fill her/his lack via a series of identifications which can never lead to a stable identity. Identities are always fragile, fluid, ever changing. In such a situation prevailing authoritarian ideologies can attract those who have a desperate need for a stable anchoring, for a permanent suturing of the desire for a stable identity. In a more general way, both the desire for a lost full jouissance and for a stable identity expresses the craving for a "fullness" which can never be achieved. The Lacanian oriented theorists Stavrakakis and Chrysoloras (2006) use both the concepts of jouissance and identification in an attempt to explain Greek chauvinistic nationalism during the last two decades. According to Stavrakakis, the Lacanian perspective provides a non-reductive way of linking the *psychodynamic* with the *social*. Their perspective focuses on the subject's lack and her/his desire for a return to a lost fullness, whereas "identification" leads us to the study of the construction of identities via the analysis of ideologies. Something similar is implied by Slavoj Zizek who, when dealing with issues of violence (2009), argues that one should study the subject on two levels: The psychoanalytic level which entails concepts such as those of jouissance, lack, suture etc.; and the discursive ("symptomal") level which focuses on textual analysis, the construction of ideologies etc.

This type of theoretically worked out articulation between the psychoanalytic jouissance and the social/cultural ideologies is a useful step forward. It is different

---

[18] On the way Lacan uses the concepts of identity and identification and their relevance for the analysis of politics, see Stavrakakis 1999.

than the "list of factors" approach which I mentioned in the previous section. But a more systematic and detailed *contextualisation* is still needed. A contextualisation which leads to the exploration of how the articulation between the psychodynamic and the social is achieved by specific collective actors or interest groups, specific institutional arrangements, specific historical trajectories. In other terms, the social cannot be limited to the study of ideological discourses and the construction of identities.

Conclusion

The chapter, by focusing on Islamic fundamentalism, has argued that what distinguishes fundamentalism as a modern phenomenon is not only the use of modern technologies (material and organizational), but also and primarily the social structure of fundamentalist regimes or social movements. More specifically it was shown the isomorphy or the elective affinity between modernity's unique sociostructural features (mobilisation/inclusion into the national centre, top-down differentiation and widespread individualization) and fundamentalism's equally unique characteristics. It is only in this way that fundamentalism as a *modern* phenomenon can be distinguished from pre-modern theocratic regimes and authoritarian religious movements. In order to show the centrality of the unique sociostructural features of modernity for the exploration of fundamentalism, I have examined the phenomenon on three levels: the cultural, the sociostructural and the psychodynamic.

Chapter 4

Modernity and Ethical Issues: MacIntyre's Three Moral Discourses

Alasdair MacIntyre's writings have shaped core, ongoing debates in moral philosophy. He rightly argues that moral theory should not be limited to discourses which operate on a highly abstract level. There should be a constant reference to social processes, to a constant interchange between moral discourses and moral actions; or, in other words, between the second order discursive practices of theorists/philosophers and the first order moral orientations and practices of laypersons (2007: 61). Given this emphasis, I will try to explore how his famous typology of the three basic moral discourses the encyclopaedic, genealogical and traditional relate to present-day, late modern social realities.

A Brief Exposé of MacIntyre's Theory

In his three major works (1988, 1990, 2007), Alasdair MacIntyre (AM) aims at overcoming the shortcomings of today's main ethical/moral discourses. His first critique is against what he calls the "encyclopaedia" approach, an approach to morality which, in Kantian fashion, is characterized by a contextless rationality: via a logico-deductive analysis one attempts to establish trans-historical and trans-cultural moral principles which are supposed to apply universally under pre-modern, modern and late-modern conditions. His major argument here is that moral principles are always context-bound; and so are the notions of rationality and justice. To ignore context space and time-wise (as moral theories from the enlightenment up to the present do[1]), leads to "fragments", to bits and pieces which fail to relate to an overall framework. They are therefore incommensurable to each other. It is precisely for this reason that moral debates tend to be "unsettleable", they lead nowhere (2007: 8).

A second discourse criticized by AM is the genealogical; a discourse which rejects encyclopaedism but offers a (non-)solution which is nihilistic and/or relativistic. From Nietzsche to Foucault, genealogy considers moral discourses as masks which hide the "will to power". Therefore, from a genealogical point of view, social theories in general and moral theories in particular can only be assessed properly not by truth but by power criteria. Given the prevalence of this discourse today, according to AM, it is not surprising that what he calls *intuitionism* or *emotivism* (2007: 16-35) reigns supreme: both on a theoretical and

---

[1] As, for instance, in the work of Rawls (1971).

a practical level one finds the belief that it is not possible to link in a rational manner the factual with the normative, the "is" with the "ought to". The choice, therefore, between conflicting moral theories and moral ways of life is less a matter of reason and more a matter of a subject's emotions or intuitions.

Contra the genealogical approach, AM argues that it is possible to link in a rational manner the factual with the normative; and contra the encyclopaedic orientation, this linkage can only be done if, following the Aristotelian and Thomist traditions, one adopts a *teleological* perspective a perspective which tries to establish in a context-sensitive manner "what is good for me". Once this is established, it is possible to view moral conduct as an effort to pass from what the subject does or *is* to what he/she *should do or be*. This passage, given the establishment of a contextually derived *telos*, is neither arbitrary nor emotive. How can one establish a subject's telos? AM provides an answer by developing a discourse based on the key notions of practices, internal goods, virtues and the unity of the narrative self in the context of a community's ongoing traditions.

By *practices* AM means "any coherent and complex form of socially established cooperative human activity through which goods inherent to that form of activity are realized in the course of trying to achieve those standards of excellence which are appropriate to, and partially definitive of, that form of activity, with the result that human powers to achieve excellence, and human conceptions of the end and goods involved are systematically extended" (2007: 187).

As the above quotation makes clear, *internal goods* are achieved in a non-instrumental manner. One enters the practices internal goods are linked to, not for the sake of external rewards (money, fame, power), but for their intrinsic value, as well as for their contribution to the welfare of other individuals who are involved in the same practices. To put it differently, whereas external goods are always some individual's property/possession and entail zero sum competition, the achievement of an internal good entails benefits for all those who participate in the practice (2007: 190). For example, if I am involved in the practice of doing research in the social sciences and my purpose is less to acquire fame or money (external goods) and more to advance knowledge as well as to contribute to the cohesion and proper functioning of the research team, then I strive towards the achievement of internal goods.

Internal goods are obviously linked to *virtues*. The latter are acquired human qualities or excellencies which help one to achieve internal goods. They also help in a more general way to sustain the quest for my telos, for what is good for me (2007: 191). Taking our previous example, as I enter the space of research practices, I try to acquire the standards of excellence required by the situation. I gradually learn the *techne* of doing research. I improve my research techniques, I gain more expert knowledge and thus I achieve internal goods such as substantial research findings, a contribution to the scientific standing of the research team to which I belong, self-fulfilment etc.

Given that I am involved in several practices as a family member, a church goer, a cricket player etc, it is my community's ongoing traditions which shape, reshape and integrate such practices transmitting them to future generations. From this point of view, as an individual I do not choose the communal and traditional contexts in which I find myself. They existed before me and they probably will go on existing after my death. In other terms, socio-historical contexts are *factual* givens which I have to take into account in trying to find my telos, i.e., what is good for me. Finally, concerning my life trajectory, this, according to AM, has a narrative character. My social world is constituted of narratives which concern my past, present and future life. Given that human beings are story-telling animals, they constantly narrate stories about themselves and about others. In social constructivist terms, the social world is symbolically and interpretatively constructed via narratives. I would add that social/moral theories can be seen as second order narratives or interpretations narrating or interpreting laypersons' first order ones[2]. From this point of view, MacIntyre's work is a narrative about other people's narratives.

As to the *unity of my narrative life*, it is achieved by taking into account practices, virtues, communal values and ongoing traditions; as well as by trying to establish, on that basis, the unity of my life or rather "the unity of a narrative embodied in a single life. To ask 'what is good for me' is to ask how best I might live out that unity and bring it to completion" (2007: 218).

All the above do not mean of course that the moral subject always aims at acquiring or always succeeds in acquiring internal goods in all the practices into which he/she is involved. Neither does it mean that he/she succeeds in the quest of "what is good for her/him", or that he/she always accepts communal values. There is no determinism involved in MacIntyre's analysis. But the fact that the subject is not seen as an "unencumbered" self but as a person who is aware of communal norms and operates within specific socio-cultural contexts renders her/his decisions non-arbitrary.

The Integration of Practices: Horizontal and Vertical

What I would like to argue in this section is that the integration of practices via the unity of the narrative life has, under late-modern conditions, not only a "horizontal" but also a "vertical" dimension and this in the sense that certain of a subject's practices develop and are integrated predominantly on the local level, others on the national and still others on the global level.

Let me start with the local level. A subject X may be a member of a local group whose major purpose is the beautification of her/his village (e.g., tending to the communal gardens, looking after old buildings etc). Such a practice entails internal goods such as being solidary with people who have similar concerns, improving the quality of communal life, feeling satisfaction for doing something useful for the community etc. It also entails specific virtues/excellencies such as developing gardening skills as well as capacities for cooperation. As AM points out, subject X is involved in other local practices as a family member, chess

---

[2] For the development of this point, see Mouzelis 2008: 84 and 178-183.

player, church goer etc, each of these additional practices entailing internal goods and virtues. How are all the above practices integrated? Via the community's ongoing traditions as well as, on the individual level, by the unity of the narrative life.

Moving now to the nation-state level, modernity is primarily characterized by a state apparatus which is radically different from all pre-modern states. Given new material and administrative technologies, it penetrates the periphery of a social formation to a degree that was impossible in pre-modern situations. This unprecedented penetration gradually reduces the self-containment of the local, traditional community and brings gradually the whole population into the national centre.

In such a situation, the self acquires not only locally-focused but also nationally-focused identities; he/she becomes a full member of what B. Anderson (1991) has called the "imagined community" of the nation-state; imagined community in the sense that it constitutes an all-inclusive whole whose members feel solidary despite the fact that they do not know each other in a direct, interpersonal manner. AM argues that the nation-state is not a community or rather that when it is viewed as such, it tends to acquire totalitarian forms. Moreover, according to him, patriotism in the modern liberal state, unlike the moral attachment to the traditional political community, cannot be considered a virtue since today "government does not express or represent the moral community of the citizens, but is instead a set of institutional arrangements for imposing a bureaucratized unity on a society which lacks genuine moral consensus" (2007: 254). He is obviously wrong. Neither the nation-state as an imagined community necessarily entails totalitarian features, nor is political attachment to modern government always based on a society which lacks moral consensus. Both in the early modern era of rising nationalisms as well as in the contemporary world, patriotic attachments can be as widely shared and as strong as those found in traditional communities. The millions of English people who were prepared to die in order to defend their country's independence during World War II had widely-shared, genuine, patriotic feelings. Moreover, the imagined community of the nation-state, like the local community entails practices, internal goods and ongoing traditions which are integrated by an individual's virtues and her/his unity of narrative life.

Let's return to our previous example. X is not only involved in local community affairs. He/she is also involved in national practices, entailing activities such as commemorating past victories and other events which have shaped the fate of the nation (Billig 1995). X is also involved, as a member of a profession, in the creation and organization of a national trade union whose major goal is the defence of its members' interests. Here as well, we see practices entailing internal goods (defence of professional interests) and virtues (increasing loyalty to the profession). In view of the above, X's narrative life is marked by "story-telling" on both the local and national level. Space-wise, it has both a horizontal and a vertical dimension. Whether local practices and identities are stronger than national ones has to do with the degree of a local community's autonomy *vis-à-vis* the national community.

Moving finally to the so-called "global village", X is an activist belonging to a global NGO whose aim is to detect and prevent human rights violations (torture, genocide, war crimes) on a planetary level. Here as well we have a much broader imagined community entailing globally-oriented practices, virtues, internal goods and ongoing traditions related to such an all-encompassing social formation. We also have practical actions and second order discourses/moral codes based on the notion of human rights and democratic liberties.

All the above imply that in late modernity the self is shaped not only by local-communal but also by national and global narratives. Needless to say, the three types of narratives are closely interrelated. They are not kept in separate compartments. Each type of discourse/narrative influences the other two. Therefore, the unity of the narrative life is achieved by taking into account practices, virtues and ongoing traditions on all three levels. To put it in non-MacIntyrean terms, the subject under late-modern conditions acquires not only locally shaped identities but also national and global ones. She/he faces the complex task of integrating her/his various identities (in space-wise terms) both horizontally and vertically (Robertson 1989).

The need to focus not only on the community but also on the national and global levels is quite obvious if one takes into account that under globalizing conditions the local, traditional community loses its self-contained character. It gradually becomes detradionalised. It is true of course that the so called *glocalisation*[3] process, by giving new impetus to old localities and/or by creating new communities, to some extent, disconnects them from the national centre. However the practices, internal goods and values of such communities are, obviously, profoundly shaped by global forces. They cannot therefore be studied in isolation. Given the above, to focus exclusively on the communal/local level leads to a "utopian" analysis i.e., to an analysis which has very little to do with present day social realities. To put it differently, the decline of what Gellner (1969) has called *segmental localism* (economic, political, cultural) is irreversible. The highly autonomous/self-contained community (which is at the basis of MacIntyre's theory) is, under late modern conditions, a thing of the past. A normative theory which claims to be based on both philosophical and social/sociological considerations cannot afford to ignore the vertical linkages between the local, the national and the global.

Globalization, Human Rights and the Euro-Centrism Issue

The existence of global narratives raises the issue of the existence of global values, particularly those related to the notion of universal human rights. AM's rejection of the encyclopaedic moral discourse is mainly based on the idea that there are no

---

[3] The neologism glocalisation sensitises the student to processes of creation or profound transformation of local communities by global mechanisms. It also points to individuals, organisations and social networks which operate simultaneously on the local and supranational level often bypassing the national level (Robertson 1994, Wellman 2002, Hampton & Wellman 2002, Sarroub 2008).

universal values; whether one looks at the notions of justice, rationality or democratic freedoms, these are always context-bound. It is therefore, according to AM, misleading to refer to them in a contextless, abstract manner. Equally misleading are moral philosophers' attempts to constitute, via logico-deductive means, universally valid moral codes. With the development, however, of a rapidly globalizing economy, polity and culture, one should raise the question of whether the encyclopaedic approach is as irrelevant as AM implies.

Let us look at values related to the human rights issue. The standard objection of those who, like AM, look suspiciously at human rights discourses, is that they are western-specific. They were developed in the West and are imposed on other cultures by imperialist powers keen to promote their economic and/or geopolitical interests (Douzinas 2000). This type of cultural imperialism thesis, as in the case of patriotism, occludes rather than clarifies the issue. It is true, of course, that values related to human rights discourses are not universal in a platonic sense. In simple, non-differentiated societies where subjects are submerged in extended kinship groups and where individuation is weak or non-existent, individual human rights are irrelevant. It is also true that the ideas of democratic liberties and human rights, although existing in a fragmentary fashion in other civilizations, were fully institutionalized in the West in the sense that civil, political and socioeconomic rights gradually, for the first time in human history, spread to the bottom of the social pyramid[4].

It is, finally, also true that the human rights discourse has been and is still used in an instrumental, ideological fashion. But in late modernity, due partly to rapid globalization processes, human rights *tend* to appeal to the majority of people who live in post-traditional contexts. Due to high levels of individuation, subjects in such contexts not only accept, but strive to achieve democratic liberties; and this, irrespective of whether they live in different cultures or in different political regimes. Whether in dictatorial China, authoritarian Mexico or democratic UK, human rights discourses have an increasing massive appeal to people living in large urban centres. And this appeal will further increase as, due to rapid urbanization, the majority of the planet's population will soon be living in post-traditional, mega cities. It is in that sense that values related to human rights tend to become universal or rather quasi-universal.

It is not therefore surprising that, as Risse and Sikkink (1999) have pointed out, human rights discourses tend today to have a "taken for granted" quality. They have acquired a "naturalness" or obviousness which was absent in the past. If we consider for instance the type of globalization which occurred during the 1860-1914 period, global socioeconomic, political and cultural mechanisms did not have great "penetrative" power. They were unable to reach the peripheries of nation states. It is only in the post-1970 globalization that, given a new institutional framework and new communication technologies, the global penetrates the national and the local in a profound manner. Because of this, human

---

[4] For the development of civil, political and social rights, see Marshall 1964 and Mouzelis 2008: 43-54.

rights narratives and institutions have had a serious impact not only on the elite but also on the non-elite, popular level. (Risse & Ropp 1999)[5].

Stepping Stones Towards Sociocultural Interpenetration

AM constantly refers to the incommensurability of such notions as rationality or justice in different cultural contexts. For him, there is not one justice nor one rationality, but several ones (1998). This argument would be valid in a world where cultures and societies were totally self-contained units. If one looks at the actual world however, one realizes that there is a growing interpenetration which is already evident in pre-modern times and which is accentuated in geometrical fashion at present. This interpenetration leads to a quasi-universalisation of certain values and notions referring to social justice and rationality.

The above becomes clearer if we view processes of growing interdependence or interpenetration from the perspective not of *specific* but of *general* evolution[6]. Let me point out in an illustrative manner some of the key turning-points or institutional breakthroughs that have led to the present extraordinary "compression" of world time and space and to the unprecedented fusion and interpenetration of cultural traditions.

- Starting from the city-states of antiquity, not only in Mediterranean Europe but also in Mesopotamia and Asia Minor, these miniscule socio-cultural formations were embedded in larger cultural-civilizational wholes that extended far beyond a specific city-state's walls and its military-administrative organization (Mann 1986: 190-231). The tendency of cultural values and norms to transcend specific juridico-administrative entities was dramatically reinforced by the shift from local, primitive religions to the so-called historic or world religions, which developed quasi-universal discourses; discourses whose abstraction made them "detachable" from local, particularistic conditions, this increasing their appeal to millions of people across a variety of societies, polities and civilizations[7].

- According to Immanuel Wallerstein (1974) it was in the sixteenth and seventeenth centuries that the first "world system" came into existence: a system of various states competing with

---

[5] For the human rights debate between "universalists" and cultural relativists, see Ishay 2004.
[6] For the concepts of general and specific evolution, see Sahlins and Service 1960.
[7] Auguste Comte is one of the first classical theorists to focus on the linkage between the growing "abstraction" of religious belief (in the move from animism to polytheism and monotheism) and the decline of cultural localism (Comte 1976). The linkage between growing differentiation and the emergence of free floating, disembedded religious ideas and values constitutes a central theme in the works of Parsons (1977) and some of his disciples, e.g., Eisenstadt (1963).

each other in the international economic, political and cultural arenas. What was unique about this system was that no one state was strong enough to undermine inter-state economic and politico-military competition by establishing an imperial order. This system was, of course, very much strengthened in the eighteenth century by the emergence of the nation-state and the shift from an inter-*state* to an inter-*nation-state* world system.

- Another crucial breakthrough during the process of growing sociocultural interpretation was the development of industrial capitalism in the 18th and 19th century Western Europe. The expansion of the nation state together with the entrance of capital into the sphere of production (agricultural and industrial), destroyed the traditional localisms of the pre-capitalist era (Dobb 1968).

- The global process of democratization after the collapse of the Soviet Union although often superficial, extremely uneven and *certainly not irreversible* is another fundamental mechanism that is bringing late-modern societies closer together on the level of political, social and cultural values (Diamond & Plattner 1996).

Summing up: world religions in the cultural sphere, the system of nation-states and the post-soviet trend of global democratization in the political sphere, the massive entrance of capital into production in the economic sphere all these, as well as the technologies with which they are inextricably linked, have brought a situation that is the exact opposite of total and cultural insulation. Therefore, today's situation creates conditions that encourage the gradual spread and acceptance of the core values of late modernity values such as productivity and competition in the economic sphere, democracy and human rights in the political sphere, and individual autonomy/self-realization in the cultural sphere. The above values, as I have argued already, are certainly not trans-historical or universal, but they do appeal to the growing number of people who live in post-traditional modern contexts. It is precisely because the above values are gradually becoming global that it is possible to transcend relativism and condemn the violation of human rights, whether this occurs in Iran, Turkey or China.

Taking the above into account, a moral discourse which takes human rights seriously cannot be dismissed in cavalier fashion as ahistorical and context-free. The context here is the global "imagined community". In such an all-inclusive context, the universally-oriented, encyclopaedic approach is relevant. It might have been less relevant in pre-modernity or in the early enlightenment period, but it becomes increasingly so at present. Today there are, as AM argues, different rationalities or notions of justice in local communities and in situations where discourses on justice, rationality or democracy are used for the promotion of interests economic, political, geopolitical. But the vision of one rationality and one justice is gradually, *at least as a vision*, emerging in the post-traditional, globalized world. Given this, moral theory, as a second order discourse, cannot but take seriously into account the globalization of moral values as these are, for instance, emerging in the practices of a young generation which, via participation in the rapidly growing new social movements and global and electronic media, is concerned with the issues of global poverty, environmental degradation and violations of human rights wherever they occur.

To conclude, given the present-day growing interpenetration of societies and cultures, it is no longer possible to reject the encyclopaedic type of moral discourses. Late modern moral theories should take seriously into account not only the horizontal but also the "vertical" dimension of practices; the fact that subjects participate simultaneously in *locally*, *nationally* and *globally*-oriented practices which all entail different internal goods, virtues, and ongoing traditions. Given this, instead of rejecting the Kantian or Rawlsian type of moral theorizing, one should focus on the complex ways in which practices articulate the local, the national and the global. One should also focus on the way in which subjects integrate such practices via the construction of a unitary narrative self. This means that context-sensitive and trans-cultural moral theories, under late modern conditions, may not be as incompatible as AM believes in which case the issue is to explore the conditions under which tradition is more relevant than encyclopaedia and vice versa.

Power Structures and Genealogy

In dealing with communities and their ongoing moral traditions, AM ignores their power structure. Although he talks about imperialism, exploitation etc. in general, when he refers to traditional communities, issues of domination disappear. This omission weakens his critique of the genealogical type of enquiry. If in the previous two sections my emphasis was on the subject's locally, nationally and globally-oriented practices, in this section I will focus on the differentiation of practices along class lines. Let us take as an example the medieval autonomous city state a case very close to the examples given by AM. Florence, in the 14th century for instance, exhibits a tripolar class system comprising the *popolo minuto* (artisans, workers, shopkeepers), the *popolo grasso* (rich employers/merchants) and the *grandi* (nobility) (Rubinstein 1997). Therefore, within the same community we have, class-wise, different versions of internal goods and virtues, different ongoing traditions, different notions of justice; or, to put it differently, within the same communal context different groups of people, because they hold different amounts of economic, political, social and symbolic capital, interpret practices differently (Frazer & Lacey 1994: 283-305).

As a result moral codes tend to differentiate along class lines. Quite obviously, for instance, the morality of the *popolo minuto* was or could be different from the *grandi's* moral outlook. Such differences might have been latent at peaceful times when the powerless accepted their position as divinely ordained. In such situations, moral elements common to the whole community might prevail. But at more difficult times, class differences and clashing moral codes tend to come to the surface. In the former case, Gramsci would talk about the upper classes imposing an ideological, cultural hegemony over the rest of the population; whereas Foucault would argue that behind the *grandi's* dominant discursive and non-discursive practices is hidden the will to power. In the latter case, common practices weaken or disappear and class conflicts tend to lead to different moral prototypes, different visions of what moral life should be. Can the moral philosophers in such cases ignore the genealogical approach? Obviously not.

Needless to say the Nitzschean/Foucauldian approach, when it claims that in *all* situations common moral codes are epiphenomena hiding the underlying will to power is both reductive and crude. It is as dogmatic as the opposite position which ignores the impact that an unequal distribution of power has on practices within communities such as the ancient Greek polis or the medieval urban community.

The above leads me to suggest that to the distinction between "is" and "ought to be", between "what people do" (the *practical* dimension) and "what they ought to do" (the *normative/moral* dimension) one should insert a third dimension; the one that refers to "what people believe or say they do" (the *ideological* dimension). In fact, if one introduces the ideological/legitimizing element between the practical/factual and the moral/normative, then we have a three-dimensional conceptual framework which leads to a less idealistic, more realistic analysis of practices. It also leads to the idea that instead of viewing AM's three moral discourses as incompatible /incommensurable to each other, one should view them as referring to different levels and contexts, in which case the issue is less to examine which is rationally superior and more to explore how *genealogy*, *encyclopaedia* and *tradition* relate to each other and to the actual practices they refer to.

Teleology and the Unity of the Narrative Life

As already mentioned, one of the major goals of AM's moral theory is to overcome the divide between "is" and "ought to be", a divide that the post enlightenment tradition considers unbridgeable. It is this belief in the impossibility of moving from the factual to the normative that leads to *emotivism*, to the idea that there is no rational way of choosing one's moral goals; no rational way of moving from what one is to what he/she should be or become. This impossibility implies that decisions on moral goals can only be based on a subject's emotions, feelings, intuitions thus leading to moral relativism.

For AM, a contextually sensitive moral theory can avoid the above arbitrariness, it can bridge the gap between the "is" and "ought to be" if one takes seriously into account the socio-cultural context: the community within which one lives, its ongoing traditions, as well as the course of the self's life narrative. By taking the above into account, the subject can answer the question "what is good for me?" in a non-arbitrary, non-emotivist, rational manner; and if this decision is not arbitrary, neither is it simply given, fixed once and for all. As AM puts it, "what is good for me is the continuous quest of what is good for me"[8]. This argument avoids circularity because a community constantly evolves and so do, via dialectical debate, its moral discourses and traditions. Therefore, the moral is always on the move so to speak. In such a situation, emotivism is avoided, since changing contextuality provides an equally changing telos. Moreover, moral theories can increasingly become more rational in the following sense: in quasi-Khunian fashion, a theoretically-oriented moral theory may generate problems which cannot be resolved within the prevailing paradigm; or two theories may be in conflict with each other. Out of this conflict a new paradigm may emerge which can lead to a rationally superior theory. This was, according to AM, the case with the Aristotelian and the Augustinian moral perspectives. Aquinas, knowing in depth the two theoretical traditions, managed to provide a synthesis which transcended their impasses (MacIntyre 1990: 115ff).

I think that AM's attempt to link the factual with the normative via a contextually derived telos, is quite convincing. It does avoid the often-arbitrary character of contextless, trans-cultural moral theories. What is more problematic however, is that his contextually sensitive theory does not take into account an actor's *internal* context or environment[9]; i.e., the socio-psychological space of self-self-inner narratives or conversations [10]; inner conversations which are relevant for understanding a subject's moral trajectory. To put it in AM's vocabulary, given the capacity for high self-reflexivity that subjects portray in post-traditional contexts, telling stories to oneself is as crucial as telling stories to others. A subject's inner world constitutes a context which entails *internalized* communal values and traditions. Therefore, the interrelations between values and norms of a specific actor's external social environment and her/his internalized values/norms should not be ignored. A subject's telos is shaped by both external and internal contexts.

The neglect of internal narratives and contexts creates problems for AM's overall theory. The non-consideration of self-self-relations eliminates cases where moral ends and means to achieve them are established in a non-decisionist, non-rationalistic manner: the telos, the quest of "what is good for me" may be pursued by means which, without being irrational, are less based on cognitive operations. In such situations ends and means *emerge* when in a negatory fashion one eliminates such obstacles as calculations, rationalizations etc. For instance, in the mystical traditions of all major religions (which AM dismisses in cavalier

---

[8] The quest for the good "is not at all that of a search for something already adequately characterized, as miners search for gold or geologists for oil. It is in the course of the quest and only through encountering and coping with the various particular harms, dangers, temptations and distractions which provide any quest with its episodes and incidents that the good of the quest is finally to be understood" (MacIntyre 2007: 2-9).
[9] For the concept of the internal environment and its linkage with external environments of action, see Alexander 1998: 215ff and 2003, Mouzelis 2008: 67-72 and 78-85.
[10] For the concept of inner conversations, see Archer 2003.

fashion[11]) as well as in post-modern anti-foundationalist ethics[12], moral rules are not supposed to derive from sacred texts, traditions or rational analysis of the Kantian contextless type or the MacIntyrean context-sensitive one. What one ought to do emerges spontaneously once one puts aside *obstacles* which prevent the open-ended self-self and self-other communication. *The obstacles consist not only of "passions" and emotions, but also and primarily of thinking, planning, being involved in means-ends operations.*

To give a concrete example, in the Christian orthodox theology, the notion of *apophatism* plays a central role. Apophatic in Greek means negatory and cataphatic is the opposite. Apophatism (which has similarities with the *via negativa* in Western Christian theology) entails two basic notions. The first is that the divine, in its *essence*, is absolutely transcendental and therefore unknowable. Secondly, the divine's *energies*[13] are, however, approachable apophatically, via emptying the self, via getting rid of or peripheralising all thoughts, concepts, images. It is by such negatory practices that the subject becomes an *"empty vessel"* ready to receive divine grace[14] (see Chapter V).

The creation of an inner void via various meditative practices one finds, of course, in many other religious traditions (Jewish, Islamic, Buddhist etc.). In a more secularized form, such practices are spreading rapidly in all late modern societies often in a form disconnected from the belief systems which have generated them in the first place[15]. One should also mention here psychoanalysis which has strong apophatic elements; and this in the sense that the analyst does not tell the analysed what to do or "what is good for her/him". Instead, with the help of the former, the latter explores and tries to transcend obstacles (e.g., repressive or defensive mechanisms) which prevent the spontaneous emergence of her/his genuine goals.

The apophatic logic is also relevant not only in self-self, but also in self-other relationships. As I explain in the next chapter, Martin Buber, the Jewish philosopher for instance, rejects in an anti-foundationalist manner all attempts at establishing moral codes via divine revelation, tradition or logical/rational analysis. According to him, the moral emerges spontaneously when in the self-other encounter one is completely open to the other, when one avoids

---

[11] According to MacIntyre, Ekhart's theology and later Heidegger's ontology lead to mysticism and to irrationalism (1990: 166ff). MacIntyre's excessive rationalism however, leads him to an under-emphasis of the existential dimensions of moral and spiritual life; it also leads him to confuse the mystical with the irrational. Despite his emphasis on contextuality, he does not take into account that certain contexts require decision-making, reason, will whereas other contexts (meditation, contemplation) require not the destruction of reason but its bracketing, its deactivation.
[12] See, for instance, Bauman 1993.
[13] The fundamental distinction between divine essence and divine energies one finds in the writings of many fathers of the Eastern Orthodox Church. Gregory Palamas however has dealt with it in a more systematic and elaborate manner (Lossky 1944: 68).
[14] For the negatory, apophatic elements in several eastern religious traditions, see Parkes 1990 and Loy 1992. For the relationships between reflexivity and the apophatic/cataphatic distinction, see Mouzelis 1999, 2001 and 2010.
[15] See on this point Heelas et al. 2005 and Roof 2001.

dissimulations, calculations, instrumental, means-ends reasoning. In such an open-ended interaction the ethical emerges. The subject knows exactly what to do or rather what he/she should do, what is the morally appropriate way of relating to the other. General moral codes extraneous to the self-other encounter are not helpful since each encounter has a unique, unrepeatable quality (1947 and 1952) (see Chapter V, third section).

All the above considerations concerning self-self and self-other relations may have been less relevant at the time of Augustine or Aquinas, but are extremely important in late modern, post-traditional contexts contexts within which reflexivity and individualization have reached unprecedented levels. Thus, one can argue that under late modern conditions one can have moral guidelines which are neither emotivist nor rationally derived. They are not arbitrary either since they spontaneously emerge from a self-stripped from rationalizing inner practices.

Needless to say, the apophatic way to morality is presented above in an ideal typical manner. But so are the three moral discourses examined by AM. In actual life, moral deliberations and practices contain elements of several discourses. A subject in her/his quest for her/his telos may be influenced by ongoing traditions in AM's sense, by principles that he/she considers universal in the encyclopaedic sense, and/or by insights reached by apophatic/meditative practices.

Conclusion

Macintyre has persuasively argued that moral philosophers should abandon their exclusively abstract, contextless theorizing; that they should link, in a systematic manner, moral theories to the socio-cultural contexts within which moral practices are embedded. On the other hand, I think that he has seriously misunderstood key dimensions of late modern realities, dimensions relevant to his analysis. It is in three areas that his analysis creates more problems than it solves.

> i. In criticizing the encyclopaedic type of moral enquiry, which attempts to establish universally valid moral codes, he does not take seriously into account that certain values (e.g., human rights) do tend to become quasi-universal. Under late modern, globalizing conditions such values appeal to most people living in post-traditional contexts and this irrespective of the specific culture or polity in which they live.

> ii. In criticizing the genealogical type of enquiry which considers moral theories as masks hiding the will to power, he neglects the power structures of traditional communities: power structures which, under certain conditions, create forms of exploitation/domination that hegemonic moral codes conceal or legitimize.

AM argues that genealogical discourses lead to emotivism i.e., to the relativistic idea that there is no rational way of establishing moral goals/rules and that therefore, a subject's choice is, from a rational point of view, arbitrary: it depends on her/his emotions, intuitions, whims. However, in dealing with the issue of emotivism, he does not take into account that in post-traditional contexts one sees the rapid development of an anti-foundationalist mode of moral enquiry. Both on the level of theory and on that of laypersons' practices, one rejects tradition, divine revelation or rational analysis as means for finding what one ought to do or be. Instead one attempts, in a negatory manner, to eliminate obstacles which prevent the spontaneous emergence of the moral. Such a process is neither based on emotivism nor is it based on rationally derived moral codes.

Chapter 5

Self and Self-Other Reflexivity

In this chapter, by referring to mundane practices as well as to more systematic/theoretical discourses I will show the utility of focusing on the negatory, apophatic aspects of reflexivity i.e., on attempts at removing obstacles mainly thinking, decision making processes which prevent the spontaneous emergence of open-ended self-self and self-other relationships.

The term *apophatic*, as already mentioned in the previous chapter, plays a central role in the theology of the Eastern Orthodox Church. It entails the notion of negativity, negativity in its non-pejorative sense. It connotes a relation to the divine and to the self which is neither activistic, nor related to cognitively oriented means-ends schemata. Apophatic theology, which has common features with Western negative theology[1], is closely but not entirely linked with *hesychasm* (hesychia in Greek meaning quietness), a spiritual movement that was important in the late Byzantine period. Its major representative in that period was St Gregory Palamas (Meyendorff 1974).

Palamas distinguishes the *essence* from the *energies* of God[2]. In its essence the divine is unknowable, unapproachable via cognitive or any other means. Therefore one cannot say anything about what it is. At most one can say what God is not. But if the divine in its essence is absolutely transcendental, in its energies it is absolutely imminent. Human beings experiencing the divine do so less as a result of mediation via sacred texts, theology, rituals and more in an unmediated, existential, personal manner. This means that cognitively based, logico-deductive means of understanding or approaching the divine are not effective. The more one uses such means, the more one gets away from God.

The direct relationship between the human and the divine can be facilitated by various practices (such as posture, breathing, repeating the Jesus prayer) which aim at purification: at emptying or cleansing the self, at eliminating all obstacles which prevent the experience of God's energies. The process is apophatic rather than cataphatic (i.e., affirmative, wilful). It leads to the elimination not only of passions and various mundane attachments but also and mainly of all thoughts, linguistic categories or even images. Thinking, even *phantasia* (i.e., imagination) must be peripheralised, subdued otherwise one becomes "not a Hesychast but a phantast" (quoted in Ware 1986: 247). In this way the human soul becomes *kene*

---

[1] For an introduction to negative theology, see Sells 1994.
[2] One finds this fundamental distinction in the writings of many fathers of the Eastern Orthodox Church. Palamas, however, has specified in a more elaborate and theologically sophisticated manner the relationship between divine essence and divine energies (see Lossky 1944: 68).

(empty), it becomes an empty vessel ready to receive the divine grace. In its more developed form this leads to *theosis,* to the fusion of the self with the divine, an experience reported by mystics of both eastern and western religious traditions. This fusion transcends the division between the adoring and the adored, the experiencer and the experienced, the human and the divine (Evdokimov 1965: 93-95).

Therefore apophatism entails two types of negativity. The first connotes the impossibility of knowing the essence of God. The second, related one, entails an inward turning into the self in order to remove mainly cognitive obstacles and to achieve an emptiness, a void which sets the ground for the experience of the divine energies.

Reflexivity: Apophatic and Cataphatic

If we now move from the religious to the secular sphere, from theology to the social sciences, I think that the apophatic/cataphatic distinction can be useful in exploring the types of reflexivity that are marked under late modern conditions. If by individual reflexivity we mean a turning inwards, a conscious intra-action, i.e., a self-relationship, than this kind of reflexivity can take both cataphatic and apophatic forms.

In the former case, the self-self-relationship is activistic, means-end oriented. The self in a purposive manner chooses a goal and then decides on the best means of achieving it. A good example of this type of inward orientation one finds in Giddens' reflexive modernization theory (1994). As mentioned in Chapter II, according to the author in modernity the traditional stable context which helps subjects to choose from a limited number of goals and the means to achieve them tends to decline. In the emerging new context the detraditionalized[3] subject is obliged to construct "her/his own biography". S/he has to choose which goals to pursue and the means to achieve them. Taking into account the above, it becomes clear that Giddens' notion of individual reflexivity is very much culture specific. Following the protestant ethic tradition, the reflexive individual's relation to her/his inner and outer worlds is conceptualized in cataphatic, ultra-activistic terms. Subjects are portrayed as constantly involved in means-ends situations, constantly trying reflexively and rationally to choose their goals as well as the means of their realization. They are also constantly monitoring or revising their projects in the light of new information and of already achieved results. Whether the chosen goal is to get rich, become famous or improve one's sex appeal, the way in which both goals and means are selected entails a cataphatic type of reflexivity that excludes or peripherialises more apophatic, contemplative, less cognitive ways of living in a world full of choices and individual challenges.

Moving now from general theory to more applied practices, a striking indication of the growth of cataphatic forms of reflexivity is the phenomenal

---

[3] On the concept of detraditionalization, see Heelas et al. 1996.

spread of "self-help" or "do-it-yourself" manuals. Such manuals advise the subject of how to rationally achieve not only external goals (such as acquiring more economic, political or cultural capital) but also internal ones such as increasing one's self confidence, self-control, decisiveness etc. (Roof 2001: 66-67). They help her/him in other terms to construct some of the identities which constitute the self. Thus we pass from the traditional ascriptive identities of the pre-modern era to the constructed identities of the late-modern one. We pass as well from traditional, taken for granted modes of integrating such identities to post-traditional, constructed integrative modes.

However, contrary to Giddens, cataphatic reflexivity is not the only way of shaping one's own biography under late modern conditions. An *apophatic* manner of turning inwards is another major way of navigating in post-traditional settings. In ideal typical terms, in this case the turning inward aims not at doing but at undoing, not at constructing but at deconstructing[4]. It aims at weakening rather than enhancing the rationalizing, calculating, planning dimensions of the self and self-other relationship. It focuses less on purposive decision-making processes and more on getting rid of "the tyranny of purposiveness". It aims, in other terms, at experiential, unmediated relationships. Eventually, it aims at the achievement of a void within which goals and means rather than being actively chosen emerge spontaneously. Goals in the apophatic case are neither pre-given/pre-constituted (as in rational choice theory), nor externally imposed. The same is true about identity formation. Identities are neither ascriptive nor cataphatically constructed. They also emerge apophatically and so does the way they relate to each other[5].

In what follows I will consider two authors who focus on ways of following an ethical life in an apophatic manner. Contrary to Macintyre's attempt (see Chapter IV) to derive what a subject ought to do be reference to a community whose social structure and culture could be assessed cataphatically, J. Krishnamurti and M. Buber explore "anti-foundationalist" routes to the ethical

This exploration, whether it has a religious or secular orientation, takes apophatic forms. In several meditational practices for instance the subject, in an effort to "quieten the mind", merely watches the passing of thoughts with no attempt either to suppress them or to engage in inner dialogue[6]. The passing of thoughts is "like a flow of a river that meanders unconcernedly along the contours of the landscape" (Jung 1990: 233). When this meditational exercise succeeds, it leads to an empty from thoughts space within which little known aspects of the

---

[4] For the connection between Derrida's deconstruction and negative theology, see Coward and Foshay 1992.
[5] For the negatory, apophatic elements in several eastern traditions, see Loy 1992. For the variety of eastern and western mystical currents, variety which relates to different socio-religious factors, see the constructionist position of Hick (1989). For a different thesis which stresses the common experiences of all mystics, experiences which are then interpreted differently by the experiencer according to her/his social and religious background, see Smart 1965 and Harmless 2008.
[6] A similar well-known exercise focuses less on the passing of thoughts and more on the regular inward and outward movement of one's breath again in an effort to minimize the subject's incessant thought processes (Sekida 1975).

self-emerge; as well as spontaneous decisions of what to do. What is the common element in most meditational practices is that it is not via thinking but via processes leading to the suspension of thinking that open self-self and self-other relations emerge[7]. In intra-active terms, for instance, in the apophatic case the self relates to itself not in activistic, rationalistic, cataphatic terms but in terms of a more passive observer-observed mode. To use a Meadian distinction, the I does not mobilize the Me as a means of achieving a chosen goal; the I merely observes the Me[8].

Of course the type of reflexivity which aims at the suspension of thoughts is not an exclusively late-modern phenomenon. As already mentioned, it can be found in most mystical traditions of East and West; as well as in the writings of philosophers ancient and modern. But it is only in late modernity that we see a remarkable movement downwards: from religious or secular elites to the common believers or "seekers"[9].

Finally, as already mentioned, it is worth mentioning that psychoanalysis, a therapy which has spread in a remarkable way during the second half of the 20th century and after, entails strong apophatic elements; and this in the sense that the analyst is not supposed to suggest the goals that the analysand should pursue or the means of achieving them. Rather the former helps the latter to become aware and eliminate various defensive mechanisms which prevent the emergence of hidden, repressed parts of the self. Once this is achieved, life goals are not imposed from outside (i.e., by the analyst) but emerge spontaneously from within the subject's inner world. So in this case as well, we see the two major aspects of the apophatic process: the elimination of obstacles and the spontaneous emergence of goals[10]. In contrast to the orthodox psychoanalytic method, in psychotherapy

---

[7] In the Zen Buddhist tradition, for instance, meditation (zazen) aims, via techniques of posture and breathing, at achieving an internal emptiness and stillness, a state of affairs in which thinking is suspended and the self-centred individual ego is eventually dissolved. In Zen texts the term muchin means "no-mind" which in turn implies "no-ego". See Sekida 1975: 36. See also Suzuki 1949 and 1964. This comes very near to Heidegger's notion of meditative thinking (1974). Meditative thinking, in contrast to calculative thinking (which entails manipulation/domination), leads to serenity or "releasement"; an inner state which is non willed, non-purposive; a spontaneous state of affairs where thoughts emerge and follow an unpredictable path. For the connection of Heidegger's notions of serenity and releasement with Taoism and Zen Buddhism, see Stambough 1990 and Kotoh 1990. For statistics showing the extraordinary spread of eastern meditational practices (especially yoga) in the West, see Heelas et al. 2005: 137.

[8] Given that G.H. Mead's classical text (1934) is based on his student's lecture notes, the I/Me distinction is not very clearly defined. It has thus received many different interpretations. I think that the most useful one is the one that conceptualizes the I as the observer and the Me as the observed. When the subject's I tries to observe itself another I appears and the "old" I becomes me. When subsequently the new I turns again to itself, it again becomes a me *ad infinitum*. This "dynamic" interpretation of the I-Me relationship points to the impossibility of closure, to the open-ended character of a subject's intra-action.

[9] See on this point Heelas et al. 2005: 5-6.

[10] See, for example, Rehm et al. 1987. Another approach which portrays strong apophatic elements is Habermas' communicative theory (1984 and 1987). Particularly in his conceptualisation of the ideal speech situation actors manage to get rid of all obstacles (exploitation, domination, indoctrination etc) which generate distorted communication. When non distorted, open-ended, balanced communication is

and in an even more accentuated manner in techniques based on cognitive and behavioural psychology, the cataphatic elements predominate (see, for instance, Rehm et al. 1987).

As to the social sciences, when the focus is on intra-action, either the emphasis is on the cataphatic dimension of reflexivity[11] or the distinction between apophatically and cataphatically derived decisions is not made. For instance, the rational choice approach is by definition cataphatically oriented; even empirical studies of the decision-making process (for instance, in formal organisations see Simon 1961) neglect the apophatic dimension. There is always the assumption that decisions are taken via attempts at cataphatically choosing appropriate means for the achievement of predetermined goals (see Appendix II). The idea that decisions may spontaneously emerge, i.e., without conscious calculations, is not taken seriously into account[12].

Self-Self Reflexivity: Krishnamurti's Radical Apophatism

Moving now to theories which focus and deal systematically with the apophatic dimension of self-self relationships, the teaching and writings of J. Krishnamurti illustrate in a striking manner apophatic reflexivity in its *secular form*. At the age of 14, J. Krishnamurti was "discovered" in India by the clairvoyant C.W. Leadbearer and brought up as a messiah by Dr Annie Besant of the London Theosophical Society. As is usual in such cases Krishnamurti's early teachings and "divine revelations" led to the founding of a religious order with followers, rituals, funds etc. But unlike most spiritual gurus coming from the East he, after a profound existential crisis in 1927, rejected his messianic status and all the elaborate religious, organisational and institutional arrangements that went with it (Lutyens 1988).

Switching to the other extreme, he developed a secular teaching in the spiritual and ethical sphere, which is profoundly apophatic. For the post-1927 Krishnamurti, spirituality has nothing to do with beliefs, whether religious or secular. Beliefs as well as divine revelation, sacred texts etc. are more than irrelevant to those searching for a genuine spirituality; they constitute serious obstacles to such a search. For him, looking inwards becomes fruitful only when one eliminates to the utmost of one's ability not only all beliefs and preconceived ideas, but also all linguistic categories, all the concepts and conceptualizations that are acquired through a variety of socialisation processes. This purgative, negatory, apophatic internal work is a necessary precondition for the emergence of the spiritual. In other words, Krishnamurti considers *thinking* and *being* as

---

achieved, consensus among participants is not imposed by an external to the situation authority; it emerges spontaneously from within the communicative process.

[11] This is clearly the case in Giddens' notion of reflexive modernisation (1994).

[12] Needless to say in this article the depiction of apophatic in contrast to cataphatic reflexivity is done in ideal typical terms. It is however the articulation of the two elements and the weight given to each that distinguishes the one from the other.

antithetical. The more the spiritual is sought via conceptual categories and reasoning, the more it becomes elusive (1954, 1956 and 1972)[13].

Spirituality, for Krishnamurti, entails a "pathless way". It entails seeing what goes on inside the self in a wordless, conceptless, detached manner, detachment here meaning not simply setting aside all beliefs and preconceived ideas, but also, as much as possible, cleansing the mind of all thoughts, labels, words (1969). When this quietening of the mind is achieved, a fusion occurs between the observing and the observed parts of the self. Assuming that internal silence or silent observation has been achieved, what happens next? Krishnamurti's instant reaction to such a question is to refuse a definite answer, urging the questioner to find out her/himself what emerges out of inner observation or contemplation. At other times (breaking his own rule) he has suggested that what does emerge is invariably a sense of unlimited compassion towards the Self, the Other, and all creatures (1978).

It is precisely this overwhelming feeling of compassion (or love) that becomes a spontaneous motivation or (non-)guide to practical action. When in a state of compassion, one does not need to consult ethical precepts or ponder alternative courses of action neither does one have to weigh the pros and cons of alternative strategies; in short, one does not have to make conscious decisions at all. The decision-making apparatus is suspended. Decisions emerge automatically, and one knows exactly what to do both *vis-à-vis* the Self and *vis-à-vis* the Other. In this sense compassion the result of silent detached, internal observation operates like the grace of God in certain Christian traditions. In the same way that the believer, by means of apophatic, negatory cleansing renders her/himself an "empty vessel" ready to receive divine grace, so Krishnamurti tells us that silent observation of what *is* prepares one for the emergence of compassion which results spontaneously in the right kind of both intra-action and interaction. The difference between the more traditional Christian apophatic method and Krishnamurti's teaching is that for the latter the source of energy and guidance is not transcendental, but is found inside each one of us.

Let me add one last point about Krishnamurti's philosophy. He does not elevate his negatory attitude into a general principle of action. He fully admits that in everyday life there are numerous situations where one has to think, plan ahead, budget time etc. However such calculating, rationalizing aspects of action not only should be mobilised solely when it is strictly necessary, but must be suspended in the sphere of intimate, interpersonal relations. In the same way that the "care of the self" requires silent, inward contemplation, the relationship of the Self with the Other should not be based on the preconceived images or typifications that thinking more or less automatically gives rise to. Relationships should not be mediated through images accumulated in the past, through mental representations which numb the senses and allow the deadweight of the past to intrude into the living here and now. It is only when we become aware of this continuous image

---

[13] See also on this point Holroyd 1980, Schallert 1996, Rinpoche 1996 and Murdoch 1996.

building, this ceaseless classification that it is possible to go beyond it and relate to the self and to those close to us in a fresh, spontaneous, ever new and open manner.

This principle holds true not only for the self-self and self-other relation, but also for that between Self and Nature. In so far as I look at the tree outside my window through the filter of past images, I do not really see the *actual* tree. My vision is clouded by the haze of mental representations constructed in the past. My casual, absent-minded, imaged look at the tree misses what is vibrant, alive, ever-changing in the actual tree. My ability to look at myself, at my spouse, or the tree outside my window in a manner that is always new and fresh depends on my ability to set aside thought processes and typifications of myself, my spouse, the tree (Krishnamurti 1975: 107 ff).

Self-Other Reflexivity: Buber

The apophatic/cataphatic distinction is also useful in understanding the type of inward looking that individuals adopt in exploring their interpersonal relations. In a certain way this type of reflexivity relates to an in-between space between individual self-self-reflexivity on the one hand and institutional or societal reflexivity[14] on the other. For in this case the focus shifts from intra-action to interaction while the broader context does not play central role[15].

In this interaction sphere as well it is possible to distinguish, in ideal typical terms, a predominantly cataphatic from an apophatic type of reflexivity. In the former case one reflects on one's own interpersonal relationships with the intent of shaping them in a purposeful, activistic manner. This may entail the adoption of detailed techniques of how to monitor interactions, as well as of how to improve relations with significant others. As with the self-self-literature, here as well there is a huge and growing industry of guides on how to improve your relationships with your spouse, your children, your boss, your friends etc. From Dale Carnegie's classical bestseller *How to Win Friends and Influence People* (1938) to Dr. Spock's manuals of how to raise your children, bookstores' shelves are full of self-other, "how to do it" books.

---

[14] Institutional reflexivity focuses less on self-self or self-other relationships and more on institutional complexes. There is a growing literature on institutional reflexivity, particularly on institutionalized practices related to the production of knowledge. See Gouldner 1971, Ellis and Bochner 2000, Alvesson and Sköldberg 2000, Bourdieu 2004 and Bourdieu and Wacquant 1992. For the growth of institutional reflexivity in late modern work contexts, see Beck 2000. A yet another type of reflexivity (not examined here) refers to processes which deconstruct texts and then turn the deconstructing critique to the deconstructive process itself. We find this type of reflexivity in the work of Nietzsche, Heidegger and Derrida. See on this Lawson 1985.

[15] Needless to say each type of reflexivity always entails elements of the other two. The distinction between the three types is useful in that it points out where the emphasis lies. For instance Krishnamurti focuses mainly on self-self-intra-actions whereas, as I will argue below, Buber on self-other interactions.

The I-It and the I-Thou Relationship

The apophatic mode on the other hand rejects ready-made, prefabricated recipes or rationally derived ethical codes. The apophatically reflexive subject becomes aware of her/his relationships and tries to deal with them in a negatory fashion: via the elimination of obstacles which prevent the open-ended, spontaneous interaction between self and other; this leading to the emergence of more genuine feelings and attachments. This type of interpersonal openness has been extensively explored in the work of M. Buber (1937). The Jewish philosopher distinguishes between two types of relationship: the "I-it" and the "I-Thou" one. The I-it relation is based on what Weber has called instrumental rationality. The self-responds to something extraneous to it (a physical object, another person, God) in a rationalizing, calculating manner. The ultimate aim is the attainment of control/domination.

By contrast, the I-Thou relation, when applied to the "interhuman", comes very close to what Habermas has called communicative rationality. Here the Other is neither reduced to an object, nor is s/he viewed as an extension of the self. There is a type of interpersonal mutuality[16] in which each individual retains full autonomy while opening up to and deeply understanding the other's situation. It is from this in-between, interhuman space of open, undistorted communication that the ethical emerges.

In negatory, apophatic terms, the *ethical* emanates from an interpersonal situation where the rationalising, calculating, planning, utilitarian element (which transforms the Thou into It) is absent. In default of such elements the I is able, in an open-ended interactive situation, to confirm the worthiness of the Other, and to show trust by being fully *present*, i.e. by not withholding from the "meeting" or "dialogue" any part of itself. A genuine meeting, therefore, being based on an I-Thou relation, presupposes a non-instrumental/non-utilitarian confirmation of the Other, which is expressed through the Self being fully present to the interactive situation (Silberstein 1989: 129ff). Given this, any attempt to cataphatically construct rules of interpersonal conduct, via sacred texts, logico-deductive reasoning or technical, "how to do it" manuals lead to closed, stultifying relationships. Any attempt at codification, classification, typification procedures prevents the genuine meeting or dialogue, for any close interpersonal relationship as well as any concrete encounter is unique and therefore not subsumable to any general category, concept or rule. Genuine guidance emerges within rather than outside the encounter/relationship (Buber 1947 and 1952)[17.]

---

[16] Buber developed the concept of mutuality in his late work. He distinguishes I-Thou relations entailing mutuality (i.e., those between persons) from I-Thou relations that are on the "threshold of mutuality", i.e., those between the Self and Nature, or Self and God. See Silberstein 1989.

[17] It is for the same reasons that the ethical cannot be found when the I turns into itself and tries to reach self-fulment, or the divine, via solitary, hermitical types of contemplation. According to Buber, although such practices do have their legitimate place in human existence, when they become dominant, they lead away from the ethical since the *interhuman* (interactive), rather than the intra-human (intra-active), is the only way of meeting not only the Other (as Thou), but also God, the eternal

The Issue of Relativism

Given the above, it is not surprising that Buber has been accused of *moral relativism*: "Buber sees man as obligated to make a decision in a set of circumstances so unique that only he alone can decide what it is that he ought to do. This in turn leads to the type of moral anarchy where anything goes and where a Hitler type of conduct can be ethical or unethical" (Fox 1967: 160). Buber tries to answer this kind of objection by developing a theory of what intrinsically constitutes our humanity. Human beings, unlike animals, are differentiated from the natural environment; they distance themselves from it by living in a social world they themselves have constructed. This separation from nature creates a fundamental insecurity which the individual can deal with either by establishing genuine I-Thou relations, or by resorting to I-it relations, i.e., to the manipulation of other human beings in an attempt at control/domination. The first strategy results in *self-actualization* where the Self, via genuine dialogue, actualizes the unique "design" inherent in each human being. When the second, the instrumental strategy is adopted self-actualization is thwarted and an objectifying, alienating I-It orientation to life acquires permanence and solidity (although never irreversibly).

Basing himself on this kind of philosophical anthropology, Buber argues that what precludes moral relativism or moral anarchy in his system of thought is the notion of self-actualization. In the genuine meeting there is no holding back of parts of ourselves. When we are present to the Other with our whole being, then we move towards self-actualization, towards the realization of our uniqueness. From this perspective, "evil" consists of creating obstacles to genuine dialogue and to self-actualization. Evil results when via suppression, pretence, manipulation we hinder the unfolding of our unique being. "One cannot do evil with the whole soul, i.e., one can only do it through holding down forcibly the forces striving against it they are not to be stifled" (Buber 1967: 720).

So, if the good cannot be derived from the outside (God, sacred texts, rational choices) it can be found in the in-between space of the genuine meeting. It springs up spontaneously when we make ourselves *present* to the Other in the right way, i.e., in a non-manipulative, non-suppressing, not I-It manner (Silberstein 1989: 129). From this perspective the move towards self-actualization is a precondition for true dialogue as well as the outcome of such dialogue. An individual develops her/his true and therefore "good" nature by constantly striving to move from I-It to I-Thou relations. In so far as I fully present myself to the other, ethical conduct comes into being spontaneously, apophatically without the intervention of concepts, categories, formulas.

Thou (Friedman 1955: 70-76). In other words, neither sacred texts nor a rational belief in God or the "good", nor any of the meditative practices developed by various mystical traditions (East or West) can be of any value if they turn one's attention away from the in-between genuine dialogue.

The Buber-Levinas Debate

Levinas' priority to the good over the ontic, to axiology over ontology, takes various forms in his work. So he talks about the ethical being prior to the natural, about *responsible* being as coming before being, about the unique Me preceding individuality, or asserts that the prime importance of ethical over ontic individuality "is due not to participation but to facing in which each individuality is a unique me facing and faced by a unique other beyond conceptuality" (quoted in Llewelyn 1995: 137).

Therefore if Buber tried to avoid moral relativism via his concept of self-actualization, Levinas attempts to overcome the inherent indeterminacy of spontaneous reaction to the Other's demand for help by resorting to a theory on what is the inherent constituent of being human. Trying to go beyond Husserl's phenomenology and Heidegger's ontology, Levinas (1981: 138) argues that what fundamentally constitutes the Self is neither intentionality nor the state of being towards death. The self-other *asymmetrical* dimension is logically prior to both the phenomenology of consciousness and the ontology of being. The elements which constitute the moral human being are the concrete existent rather than existence in general, the "face" rather than the individual, the saying rather than the said, "fissure" rather than totality, discontinuity/disruption rather than continuity/harmony, alterity rather than sameness, asymmetry rather than symmetry, etc.

There are striking similarities between Buber's and Levinas' theories of self-other relationships. They both reject instrumental rationality and stress the fact that the ethical cannot be derived cataphatically by sacred texts, traditional codes, rationalization etc. For both, the interhuman/interactive is the space where ethical conduct emerges spontaneously. Moreover, they both oppose moral relativism by stressing that a certain opening-up to the Other constitutes our humanity, and as such is "always, already" there. It can be suppressed, but it cannot be made to disappear. It is not something to be constructed, chosen, or invented, but something to be discovered. Hence for both authors cataphatic attempts at intellectualization, codification, standardization hinder or suppress the emergence of the ethical; they lead to *thinking* rather than *doing* the good.

Of course, there are also fundamental differences between the two thinkers. Levinas (1967: 70) has criticized Buber's theory by arguing that the latter's dialogic in-between situation is too *symmetrical* in the sense that it refers more to the type of reciprocal *amitié spirituelle* of friends than to the fundamental imbalance that feeling responsible for the "hungry and naked of this world" necessarily entails. In other words, for Levinas mere confirmation of the Other's humanity is insufficient to constitute the ethical. The ethical transcends mutuality, because it necessarily entails responsibility not towards a friend or an equal, but towards an unknown, mysterious Other (Smith 1983: 108).

Buber replied to Levinas that the I-Thou relation is by no means limited to the mutual understanding and respect that friendship implies, for it refers to a kind of reciprocity between human beings who might have no shared characteristics or interests apart from their common humanity. Moreover, for Buber the idea of the ethical comprises far more than that of unconditional, asymmetrical help, in the sense that "if all were well clothed and well nourished, then the real ethical problem would become wholly visible for the first time" (Buber 1967: 723). What needs stressing from the point of view of this article is that for both philosophers the ethical relationship (whether symmetrical or not) is achieved in an apophatic, negatory manner.

Moreover, as already mentioned, both theorists try to avoid moral relativism by developing a philosophical anthropology in which a kind of openness to the Other is constitutive of the Self. This openness takes the form of mutual confirmation and trust in Buber's case, and of unconditional responsibility for the Other in the case of Levinas. This position does indeed avoid moral relativism or indeterminacy, but at the price of introducing an *essentialist* assumption based on a general, universal theory of what constitutes our "true" humanity. It is a monistic assumption which is as problematic as its opposite, which stresses the inherent wickedness of human beings and the need, not for discovering the good, but for controlling and regulating the "bad".

Conclusion

By referring to mundane practices as well as to more systematic/theoretical discourses (particularly those of J. Krishnamurti and M. Buber), I have tried to show the utility of the apophatic/cataphatic distinction in the study of self-self (intra-active) and self-other (interactive) forms of reflexivity.

The major points of my argument are:

i. Reflexivity, whether it focuses on self-self or self-other relationships can take both cataphatic and apophatic forms.

ii. In the former case the turning inwards is characterized by an activistic, purposive, goal achievement mode. The intent in this type of intra-action is, via internal deliberations, to choose a specific goal (among the many available) and then to decide on the most rational ways of achieving it.

In the self-other relationship the cataphatically oriented subject reflects on her/his relationship to the other and tries to change or improve it by following established codes, by rational analysis or by adopting techniques of interpersonal management.

iii. In the apophatic case the subject turns inwards in a negatory fashion.

In the self-self relationship this entails the elimination or peripheralisation of obstacles (rationalisations, decision-making processes, thoughts, images) which prevent the emergence of a spontaneous mode of being and acting.

In the case of self-other reflexivity the subject reflects on her/his relationship with the other with the intent of eliminating various forms of closure (typification processes, instrumental orientations to the other, concealment of parts of the self, etc.) which prevent the emergence of an open-ended form of human interaction.

iv. What is common to both self-self and self-other apophatic reflexivity is that the removal of obstacles (particularly rationalizations and thinking in general) is supposed to lead to a situation where decisions concerning everyday life rather than being purposively imposed, emerge spontaneously from within the intra-active or interactive situation. To put it differently, what is common is an openness to the self and to the other in an attempt to avoid the type of defensive closure which is one of the typical reactions to the risks and uncertainties of late modern life.

v. Given the ideal typical formulation of the apophatic and cataphatic types of reflexivity, in actual life one finds both apophatic and cataphatic elements in one's intra-active and interactive reflexive processes. In order therefore to distinguish the one mode from the other one has to assess in any specific situation which of the two is dominant. The last point suggests ways in which the apophatic/cataphatic distinction can lead to empirically oriented studies. Thus one can investigate the degree and type of emphasis given to apophatic or cataphatic reflexive orientations to the self and/or the other in specific institutional spheres (economic, social, religious, artistic, scientific), in different organizational cultures (of corporations, hospitals, schools etc); or in the norms that specific roles entail.

Chapter 6

Instead of a Conclusion
Modernity: Six Orientations to the Divine

In this final chapter, I focus on six orientations to religion and their relation to the concept of modernity as developed in Chapter II. I tried to avoid simply recapitulating the general themes of each chapter. Instead, I incorporated and at the same time developed them further with the help of a typology of orientations to the divine some of them positive, other negative and some "neutral".

In late modernity, both on the elite and non-elite level, subjects adopt different ways of relating to religion. In ideal typical terms one can distinguish six major orientations. The six orientations list is not, of course, exhaustive. But I think, as far as the linkages between modernity and orientations to the religious are concerned, the ones discussed here are the most relevant:

- Theism (theistic religiosity)

- Anthropocentrism (the "indwelling God" orientation)

- Syncretism

- Agnosticism

- Apatheism

- Atheism

Theism

Theism is based on the central belief that God has not only created the universe but also intervenes in the world and has direct, personal relationships with human beings. This contrasts with *deism* which emphasizes that God as the creator of the cosmos does not interfere with its functioning. In the theisitic case, God's intervention often takes the form of revelation which leads to the creation of fundamental sacred texts, the latter providing ethical and spiritual guidance to the believers. Therefore, a set of religious beliefs and rituals play a dominant role in the sense that they are constitutive elements upon which a religious organization or tradition is based. Such elements are usually preconditions for joining or continuing to belong to this specific religious culture. In Christianity the Catholic

Church is a good example of this type of religiosity. For instance, deviations or rejection of fundamental beliefs such as Christ's divinity are reasons for exclusion. Groups which reject major dogmas are considered "sects" not belonging to the catholic family.

With the advent of modernity this type of orientation is undergoing a process of religious rationalisation (Weber 1925: 538ff): the pre-modern chasm[1] between elite and popular religiosity is diminished. As the "means of salvation" are concentrated at the top, religious elites are more able to control what is happening at the periphery. Therefore, elements from the official, elite religiosity penetrate the social base, displacing communal traditions which often entail magical elements and other local "prejudices". In other terms, we see in this case the mobilisation and inclusion of believers from the periphery to the centre, as segmental localism declines and religious resources (material and symbolic) shift from the periphery to the religious centre.

As far as Christianity is concerned, in late modernity the process of religious rationalisation is linked with a process of secularization as the church loses some of the control it exercised over non-religious institutional spheres (educational, recreational etc.). Its intervention in other differentiated institutional spaces has not ceased; but nowadays it operates on the basis of what Rowan Williams has called *procedural secularism*[2]. It participates in the public sphere on equal terms with other secular forces or agencies. On the other hand, in *intra-institutional* terms, in the early post-war period secularization was advancing fast in the west (the United States being an exception). But from the late 60s onwards we are witnessing a religious revival both inside and outside the sphere of institutionalised religion (Glock & Bellah 1976, Beckford & Luckman 1989, Beyer 1994, Heelas & Woodhead 2005, Lynch 2007). At the same time, particularly in Latin America and Africa, evangelical Christianity is developing rapidly (Martin 2005 and 2011).

From the above it becomes obvious that modernity is not incompatible with religiosity, Christian and non-Christian. Theistic religious orientations based on elaborate belief and ritual systems will continue to be, if not dominant, at least an important constitutive feature of late modernity.

Anthropocentrism

In this case God exists *exclusively* within us. The "divine spark", at least as potentiality, comes from within rather than from above. There is no external to the subject God, creator and ruler of the cosmos. As far as Christianity is concerned, such an orientation is to be found at the extreme end of liberal Protestantism. One accepts the teachings of Christ as prophet but rejects the dominant Christian ontology on the nature of divinity (Cupitt 1980 and 1984). As all other

---

[1] For the chasm between elite and popular religiosity in several religious traditions, see Sharot 2001.
[2] On the relation between religion and the public sphere as well as on Rowan Williams' notion of procedural secularism, see Bedford-Strohm and Deane-Drummond 2011.

orientations examined here, this one is also "spreading downwards". In a very interesting survey in the UK it was found that one out of every three adults interviewed claimed that "people have God within them, so churches aren't really necessary" (Roof 2001: 85). One finds a similar, although not identical approach, in Mahayana Buddhism: an external to the subject God does not exist but buddhahood, as the divine exists within us (Williams 1991).

The anthropocentric idea of the indwelling God has an elective affinity with the *apophatic* approach to the divine[3]. Given the rejection of sacred texts based on beliefs in a divinity which has created the cosmos, moral guidance cannot come from the outside so to speak. Ethical rules cannot be derived by divine revelation or by the interpretation of the Bible, the Koran or the Vedas. They can be found within us once, in a negatory, apophatic manner we remove those internal obstacles which prevent us to commune with the divine within. Such obstacles primarily consist of thoughts, images and, more generally, processes of rationalisation which do not allow us to approach the indwelling God in a non cognitivistic manner. Once there is a move from the cognitive to the experiential, once the self is emptied from thought processes, what we "ought to do" emerges spontaneously from within. One does not need to consult holy books, ethical treatises or philosophical/theological analyses on the nature of the moral and the good. As mentioned in Chapter V, the moral way to relate to the self and the other appears without the activation of decision-making processes. In other terms, the ethical does not come from the outside; it rises from the inside once rationalising, calculating, planning etc. is suspended.

Syncretism

In pre-modernity, as Giddens (1994) has pointed out, traditional codes were providing a stable framework which reduced choices and helped people to lead their lives in a taken for granted manner. In such a situation, rules/norms on what one ought to do or not to do were provided by the communal culture and social structure. Of course, the opportunities for choice were there. But the space where decisions could be made was narrow and clearly delimited. To a considerable extent, the charting of one's life was given rather than individually constructed. In late modernity this relatively stable situation is weakening or disappearing. The subject is not only faced with a very wide range of choices in all institutional spheres (economic, political, cultural, religious), she/he is also obliged to create by herself/himself the very choice-reducing framework that tradition was

---

[3] The term *apophatic*, as mentioned in Chapter V, plays a central role in the theology of the Eastern Orthodox Church. It entails the notion of negativity, negativity in its non-pejorative sense. It connotes a relation to the divine and to the self which is neither activistic, nor related to cognitively oriented means-ends schemata. Apophatic theology, which has common features with western negative theology (Sells 1994), is closely but not entirely linked with *hesychasm* (hesychia in Greek meaning quietness), a spiritual movement that was important in the late Byzantine period. Its major representative in that period was St Gregory Palamas (Meyendorff 1974).

providing. To put it in Giddens' terms (1994), in late modernity the subject has to construct "her/his own biography"; or as Ulrich Beck has put it, he/she has to create "a life of one's own" (Beck and Beck-Gernsheim 2003). In a later work Beck (2010) argued that the same is true in the religious sphere. Given modernity's widespread individualization, one has to create a "God of one's own"; a divinity who is the result of *choosing* elements from a variety of religious traditions, elements which suit the believer's unique needs and idiosyncracy.

More specifically, with rapid globalization, as religions come closer together (Robertson 1989) and as they often interpenetrate, we see the development of religious relativism and the emergence of a "spiritual market place" (Roof 2001); a place where religiously oriented subjects are offered a multiplicity of choices as far as beliefs and spiritual practices are concerned. As individualization is spreading downwards, it is not only spiritual *virtuosi* but also people from all walks of life who turn their backs to bureaucratically organised religious establishments. They turn instead to the so called new religious movements which are mainly related to eastern religious traditions. From *Maharishi's Transcendental Meditation* to *Sai Baba's* global organization, the new religious movements proliferate. In this way, particularly among the young, "spiritual seekers" construct a "God of their own" combining hindu, buddhist, taoist etc. elements with christian ones. Moreover, religious eclectivism can also be found within established christian churches which often tolerate, for instance, Buddhist forms of meditation[4]. They also tolerate groups which are loosely linked to the church and whose members mix Christian with non-Christian beliefs (e.g., the doctrine of reincarnation) and practices (e.g., channelling).

***

Moving now from religious to irreligious or anti-religious orientations (agnosticism, apatheism and atheism), the major links between them and modernity are widespread individualization and the "movement downwards", i.e., the spread of secular orientations from the elite to the non-elite popular level. As the pre-modern, relatively self-contained, non-differentiated, traditional community is declining, the divide between centre and periphery is diminished in the secular sphere as well. Indifference towards religion, agnosticism and atheism do not anymore characterise small circles of cultural elites in the centre. They spread to people in all walks of life, people who do not necessarily have any philosophical/theological training or interest.

Agnosticism

Philosophers form Hume to T.H. Huxley and J.S. Mill have tried to provide theoretical foundations to the agnostic position. Their major argument is that

---

[4] For this type of within the Christian churches syncretism, see Heelas and Woodhead 2005.

questions about the existence of a divinity which has created the universe are unanswerable. They are beyond the capacities of human reasoning. In the above sense, God's existence can never be proved; it will remain a mystery for ever. On the other hand, in the case of what philosophers have called "soft agnosticism", it is only at present that a scientific answer is not available. The future development of science may lead to sound proofs about God's existence or non-existence. Finally, a third position related to the agnostic logic is the argument that what matters is not the God's existence issue but a certain type of spirituality which can be developed in a context within which the problems related to the existence of a divinity are bracketed (Kramer 1986). This type of "spiritual agnosticism" has taken its most extreme form in Krishnamurti's teachings and writings (1978 and 1985). For the western educated Indian sage religious beliefs in general and the belief in the existence of God in particular, are not only spiritually irrelevant, they are also profoundly anti-spiritual. They lead to sterile philosophical speculations[5]. What has reinforced spiritual agnosticism is the proliferation in the west of meditative practices which, even when derived from a specific religious tradition, are supposed to be compatible with any religious or even irreligious orientation.

Finally, one should stress here that agnosticism, like the two other secular orientations to be examined, has a long history. But in antiquity for instance, it was limited to philosophical circles[6]. It was only in modernity that the agnostic orientation spreads from cultural elites to the non-elite level.

Apatheism

In the philosophical/theological vocabulary indifference to religion is called *apatheism* (*apathia* is a Greek term connoting lack of concern or indifference). Apatheism in the Catholic Church is considered a moral failure leading to social irresponsibility and/or hedonism (Borne 1961). On the other hand, for those adapting a secular orientation, apatheism is considered positively. It is viewed as a step forward since it prevents obscurantism, fanaticism and religious violence (Rauch 2003). As to what is called *moral apatheism*, this discourse develops the argument that morality does not need religious foundations. Human beings are capable of creating and following ethical codes without help from divine revelations or sacred texts[7]. Needless to say, laypersons are not involved in theoretical, philosophical discussions on apatheism. They simply follow a course of life which entails neither religious beliefs nor practices. Concerning the latter, apathetic subjects often join religious ceremonies for aesthetic reasons (e.g.,

---

[5] This orientation relates to Gautama Buddha's refusal to discuss any metaphysical questions - reminding his disciples that his aim was not to teach about the existence or non-existence of God. His aim was to show how to overcome craving and suffering.
[6] On ancient atheism and agnosticism, see Minois 1998: ch. 2.
[7] Indifference is often the result of agnosticism: "I do not want to waist time with questions which are unanswerable"; or Diderot's famous declaration "I do not care if God exists or not".

enjoying religious music) or out of respect for tradition (e.g., going to church at Christmas).

As with agnosticism, in late modernity the indifferent/apathetic orientation to religion is also spreading widely. It is adopted by a great number of people in whose life religion plays a minimal role[8] or no role at all. From this point of view, apatheism has an elective affinity with the dominance of consumerist values, dominance intensified by the neo-liberal globalization from the late 70s onwards. Consumerist culture on the one hand and the various fundamentalisms (particularly those developed within monotheistic religions) on the other have led a great number of people to indifference or to an overall rejection of all types of religiosity. This leads us to a consideration of the atheistic orientation to the religious.

Atheism

Atheism, which also has a very long history (Minois 1998), has entered systematically the public sphere in the 18th century *lumières* culture by the *philosophes* and the anti-clericalist forces of the French revolution. (1998: ch. 11) Later Feuerbach and Marx have argued that religion is a form of alienation. Human beings construct religious ideas which at some point turn against them since they are used by the dominant classes in order to consolidate their rule. More recently militant atheism revived after the 9/11 terrorist attacks. In fact, militant atheists like Dawkins (2007), Harris (2005), Dennet (2006) and others have produced works which are bestsellers all over the globe. Particularly in Western Europe atheism is advancing fast. Statistically based studies relate educational levels with atheist orientations. Shermer (1999: 76-77) has shown that religions certainties weaken as educational levels rise. Another relevant study (Zuckerman 2009) has found a positive correlation between education and secularity (including atheism). The link between atheist orientations and educational achievement is directly relevant to the social structure of modernity.

As is well known, in pre-modernity education was limited at the top of the social hierarchy. It was only children from affluent families who had access to formal education. With the advent of modernity the right to education gradually spreads to the social base. Therefore, modernity's unique "mobilisation/ inclusionary" feature operated in the educational sphere as well. The decline of segmental localism and the state penetration of the periphery meant the spread of formal education downwards. In fact, mass education and the shifting of orientations and attachments from the periphery to the centre was a principal, if not the principal, mechanism leading to the construction of the nation state. Given the link between education and atheism, it is not surprising that atheistic orientations have an elective affinity with a modern mode of life. Needless to say, atheism, like moral apatheism, does not reject morality; it rather tries to

---

[8] On "minimal" religion, see Epstein 1999.

disconnect it from religion as the provider of the unique foundation of ethics. Militant atheists today tend to adopt a secular humanism and to stress the necessity of spreading human rights world-wide[9].

Some Remarks on the Six Orientations

- The six ways of relating to religious phenomena are *ideal types*. Most often, in concrete situations there is a mixture of interrelated elements, a configuration within which one is dominant. For instance, in the west Buddhist meditative practices and non-Christian beliefs are adopted by small groups which, however tenuously, are linked to Christian churches (Heelas & Woodhead 2005). And of course, particularly as far as the Catholic Church is concerned, in Latin America and Africa non-Christian communal traditionalism persists and infiltrates the dominant set of Christian beliefs and rituals.

- We usually link spirituality to religion. However in the recent relevant literature many authors distinguish between the two (Heelas & Woodhead 2005, Fuller 2001). I think that the distinction is useful; particularly if one is to argue, as I do, that spirituality can take both religious and secular forms. In both cases it entails a turning inwards, a discipline of body and mind, a loving/compassionate opening to self and other and a type of expanding altruism which goes far beyond correct ethical behaviour. From this point of view spirituality is, potentially or actually, an important dimension of human beings - particularly during the modern period of widespread individualization. It is a dimension analytically distinct from cognitive, ethical or aesthetic aspects of human existence.

- All six orientations can have a spiritual dimension. Thus in the theistic religious orientation, the phenomenon of "saintliness" appears in all major religions (James 1902). Saintliness is achieved by individuals who often combine beliefs and rituals with a variety of disciplines (ascetic and non-ascetic) which help them to achieve high levels of spiritual development. As to those who opt for the "indwelling God" orientation or for the

---

[9] Finally, it is worth mentioning that in terms of social ontology a major difference between atheistic and religious orientations is that the former are based on overall social constructionism whereas the latter by weak or partial one. Indeed, for atheism religious reality is in its entirety socially constructed. It is a human construct. Whereas for religious orientations, particularly christian ones, it is God as a non-constructed creator who is religion's foundation. Believers construct religious phenomena via the reception of divine grace.

syncretic one, they can obviously also reach high spirituality. As far as secular non-religious or antireligious orientations are concerned, if spirituality is defined as above, there are certainly subjects with secular orientations whose altruism, love for the self and other and intense inner life can render them highly spiritual. Needless to say, some of the six orientations and particularly those based on religious beliefs and rituals can lead to extreme fanaticism and profoundly anti-spiritual attitudes and practices. As striking examples one can think of the religious wars in Christian Europe, or Islamic fundamentalism today. In a more general way religion, as all other institutions, has a bright and a dark side. In the former case it provides the means through which human beings can develop their spiritual potential. In the latter it provides means for dogmatic closure and for anti-human, often murderous practices.

- In late, globalized modernity, contrary to what early secularization theories proclaimed, religion is not going to wither away in the medium or long term. At present, as already mentioned, there is a religious revival in the west, whereas charismatic Christianity is rapidly expanding in the Third world - particularly in Latin America and Africa (Martin 2011). Religion *is* compatible with modernity. But so are secular modes of existence. In fact all six types of orientations will be with us not only in the short and medium but also in the *longue durée*. All six are spreading and will continue to spread downwards to put it differently, religious and secular orientations will constitute permanent and important features of late modern life. There will be, of course, fluctuations in their importance but all six will continue to provide a set of different modes of existence, different life worlds from which highly individualized subjects will choose in order to construct "their own biography'.

What is important for the planet's survival, among other factors, is that the spiritual rather than the non-spiritual prevails in both the religious and the secular spheres. Genuine spirituality can unite human beings who have different orientations to religion. It *undermines* both religious and secular fanaticism. It cultivates tolerance and understanding between those who follow a religious and those who opt for a secular way of existence. It can also promote the idea that no church, no religious tradition, no secular dogma has the monopoly of truth - that there is no one but several routes to a spiritual mode of being.

Appendix I

Lacan and Meditation:
From the Symbolic to the Postsymbolic

The emergence of symbolic language enables *homo sapiens* to detach himself from the here and now, from the concrete context and immediate time of non-human existence. The passage from animal behaviour to human act (Lacan 1977: 50) enables human beings to transcend the limitations of animal communication. It allows them to think about their possible future and their certain death; it allows them to explore their inner worlds as well as to place themselves empathetically in the position of the other. It is in this way that humans transcend the animal's confinement to the here and now, that they can think about their past and imagine what will come next. Unlike animals, they create a breach between themselves and the surrounding cosmos; they are part of but also apart from it. This existential splitting, particularly in modernity, leads human beings to see themselves as being thrown into the world for reasons they are ignorant of. They march to their death without knowing what comes after it and what life is all about.

The Adam and Eve story resembles both the philosophical narrative which stresses how symbolic language cuts off human beings from the cosmos and the Lacanian theory of how language, *the symbolic*, leads the subject from full undifferentiated existence to a state where s/he experiences a lack that nothing can suture permanently. In the biblical story the eating of the forbidden fruit (which can be interpreted as the acquisition of symbolic language) leads to the fall, to an existence that creates a split between human beings and God, a split leading to sinful living and suffering.

However, in the Christian story there is hope, the New Testament hope that God's incarnation in Christ, his resurrection and the second coming, will overcome the divide between sinful and paradisiacal existence. Such a hope one does not find, of course, in the more pessimistic Lacanian discourse. The return to a full jouissance of the pre-symbolic, pre-language type is not possible not only in pathological cases (psychosis, perversion, acute neurosis) but also in the case of the "normal neurotic" subject, since the dominance of the symbolic always leads to division and alienation. In this paper I will consider the relevance for Lacanian theory of meditation practices which are spreading widely in the West and which are extensively studied in the sociology of religion today. Such practices relate to the widespread individualization which is a major feature of late modernity. In that sense, they are relevant not only in the religious sphere but also in the sociopolitical.

Language and the Symbolic

For Lacan the *real* as distinct from socially constructed reality is neither an unknowable deity (as in Christian apophatic/negative theology), nor a type of Kantian noumenon. It is the part of us which resists language; it either resists symbolisation or is non-symbolisable. In the pre-symbolic stage the real is dominant. It entails jouissance and the infant's non-differentiated, non-divided existence. After a phase in which the imaginary prevails, we have the dominance of the symbolic. The "law of the father" entails the symbolic castration and the prohibition of incest, leading to the imposition of a strictly limited access to the mother. Full jouissance and the undifferentiated real are lost if not for anything else, because of the subject's mediated relation (via language) to the real and reality. But partial jouissance persists, as the "remainder real" resists the process of symbolisation[1]. It is during this process that the division between the conscious and the unconscious appears. According to Fink (1997: 152) the unconscious is a foreign language which we cannot directly read. What is repressed is not an experience but words (that is, signifiers) to which the traumatic experience is attached. The unconscious entails symbolic elements *since it functions like a language*, a language whose codes are unknown to the subject. They form chains of signifiers which are integrated into a coherent whole via a dominant signifier (*point de capiton*). This type of formation "speaks" to the subject in a cryptic manner via dreams, slips of the tongue, reveries and other similar mechanisms.

The analyst's task, then, is to decode, to bring to the conscious surface the hidden codes and rules of the unconscious language. Therefore, contra Freud, the focus of the analyst should be less on exploring early, repressed, unknown (to the analysand) traumatic experiences and more on bringing to the surface the chain of signifiers which are linked to the analysand's various symptoms. Since any single signifier acquires its meaning when seen in its relation to the chain's other signifiers, one should explore the syntactic and grammatic rules which link one signifier with another. Such rules, following Saussure and Lévi-Strauss, consist mainly but not exclusively, in metaphoric and metonymic types of mechanisms.

The unconscious linguistic codes which are hidden to both analysand and analyst are crucial. Their exploration is a major path to understanding the ways in which unconscious subjectivity "speaks" and often orders and dominates the conscious subject. The subject, split by the conscious-unconscious divide, is driven by forces which s/he does not know and therefore does not control. If for Feuerbach (1855) societal alienation refers to forces that humans create but cannot control, the Lacanian subject is alienated by unconscious linguistic mechanisms which are unknown and therefore not controllable. If for Feuerbach (and for Marx

---

[1] Fink (1997) distinguishes Real I which entails full jouissance and Real II (the "remainder real") entailing partial jouissance. Another definition of the remainder real is to see it as an element within the symbolic sphere which "escapes symbolic closure" (Shepherdson 2008: 11). Finally, concerning full jouissance, it is only retroactively that the subject, at the symbolic stage, considers his presymbolic jouissance as having been full.

as well) alienation is reduced when human beings become aware of the distortions of social reality that ideologies produce, for Lacan the subject's alienation is weakened when s/he, with the help of the analyst, becomes aware of some of the signifiers and their linkages to her/his symptoms. When this happens symbolisation advances and the dominance of the real recedes without ever being eliminated. The subject of the partial jouissance remains forever divided and alienated[2], but consciously so; it establishes a *modus vivendi* with its own division and starts to enjoy the partial jouissance accessible to it.

Language and Mysticism

Given the central role that language, both conscious and unconscious, plays in Lacanian theory, one could raise the following question: what happens when the subject manages, via various techniques, to suspend language, to bracket words, sentences and thinking, succeeding thus in experiencing some sort of post-symbolic spiritual jouissance, a state of affairs where division and alienation seem to recede? It is this type of bracketing that spiritual elites in most mystical traditions (Christian, Jewish, Muslim, Buddhist, etc.) seem to achieve for short or long periods. The same type of experience is achieved, in a more attenuated form, via different types of meditation by subjects who do not link their meditative practices with any religious beliefs or rituals. What is common to most types of meditation is the suspension of the symbolic the suspension of language and thinking.

In other terms, if division and alienation is produced by the advent and dominance of symbolic language, is psychoanalysis the only way of attenuating the subject's alienation? Is "more language", in the form of the discursive interaction between analyst and analysand, the only way to attenuate the subject's alienation? Could it be that the achievement of "inner silence" via meditation is another way of reducing division and constant lack? It is true, of course, that Lacan, in the context of psychoanalysis, was against conscious thinking by the analysand, which he considered not effective. According to Fink (1996: 43-44), for Descartes thinking is *being*, for Lacan thinking is *rationalisation*. But the fact that psychoanalysis is mainly a "talking cure" makes it very different from meditative practices which aim at bracketing not only conscious thinking but also any type of conversation, self-self or self-other. Therefore, concerning language, one may identify two strategies: the psychoanalytic one, which registers the limits of language (Shepherdson 2008) and the meditational one, which focuses on its bracketing/suspension.

---

[2] Needless to say, Lacan's concept of alienation entails not only division within the subject but also division between subject and the other. There is a chasm between self and the other since the relationship is mediated not only by language but also by imaginary elements entailing misconception and estrangement. According to Lacan, however, alienation is also linked to creativity - since the subject's lack often leads to never-ending, often creative efforts to suture it (Chaitin 1996).

To the above, there is the objection that meditation is an epiphenomenon, a practice useful but unable to go deep enough and to explore the unconscious processes which enhance, in a more or less permanent manner, alienation. There is no doubt that the conscious-unconscious split cannot be overcome by meditation; but meditative practices, when seriously pursued, can attenuate the subject's sense of lack and division. By attenuating the alienating split, the subject becomes more aware and therefore more able to control pressures that lead to compulsive behaviour. There is also the objection that mystical experiences (union with the divine, *theosis*) may pertain to cases of psychosis or acute neurosis. But surely not all mystical experiences are pathological, since genuine mystics can shift at will from silent contemplation to a more active state: helping others, criticising (like the ancient prophets) the bureaucratisation/corruption of religious establishments, creating new religious orders, etc. (see King 1998, Louth 2007, Attwater 1965).

There is finally the argument that the mystic's union with the divine is a fantasy, since god does not exist. But union with the divine can be interpreted, as in some forms of liberal Protestantism, as union with the "indwelling divine", with an internal-to-the-subject state of affairs that certain spiritual disciplines bring to the fore, thus reducing division and estrangement. For such an anthropocentric approach the idea of the "indwelling God" means that there is no divinity external to the subject (Cupitt 1980 and 1984, Robinson 1965 and 1973). On the basis of the above, as William James pointed out, nothing can be more absurd "than to bar out phenomena from our notice, merely because we are incapable of taking part in anything like them ourselves" (1902: 120). James later observed, "psychology and religion are in perfect harmony up to this point, since both admit that there are forces seemingly outside the conscious individual that bring redemption to his life" (1902: 211).

Although some mystical experiences may be fake and/or pathological, others definitely are not. A sign of non-pathological mystical experiences entailing a genuine opening to the self and the other is "saintliness". Although a detached observer cannot understand how saintliness is achieved, it is a phenomenon one finds in most "axial" religious traditions, that is, those religions which, between 800BC and 300BC, developed a type of spirituality which was non-existent in more archaic, exclusively ritualistic religious traditions (Jaspers 1953, Armstrong 2006). They all create a space where genuine spirituality can emerge. William James, a profound analyst of various religious phenomena, argues that "there is a certain composite photograph of universal saintliness, the same in all religions the main features of which can easily be traced. They are a feeling of being in a wider life than that of this world's selfish little interests. An immense elation and freedom as the outlines of the confining selfhood melts down, and a shifting of the emotional centre towards loving and humanitarian harmonious affections" (1902: 269-270).

It is true, of course, that Lacan was interested in mysticism and its relation to the limits of language (1975). According to Lacanian theory, genuine mystical experiences (like those of Saint Theresa of Avila or of Saint John of the Cross) lead to a type of jouissance which is neither the infant's presymbolic jouissance nor the *partial jouissance* of the divided subject. The mystic, via the stripping of the self from passions, mundane desires as well as thoughts, words and even images, strives for a union with the divine. The mystic's often ecstatic, excessive, "other jouissance", as Lacan calls it, refers to the real rather than to the imaginary or symbolic order. From this point of view, despite Lacan's atheism, his writings on the real open up a door to issues of transcendence, a door that Freud kept firmly closed.

Non-Mystical Meditation

Buddhist ways of going beyond partial jouissance are less transcendental than the ways of the Christian mystics. They aim less at a union with the divine and more at overcoming desire and the miseries of everyday existence. Buddhism, at least in its early stages, was profoundly anti-metaphysical. It rejected questions about the afterlife and the divine; it set as its main goal the overcoming of what Lacan called *lack*. For instance, the historical Buddha refused to answer disciples' questions about transcendental states of being. Rather, the Buddha always reminded his followers that his aim was not to teach about the existence or non-existence of God, but how to overcome human craving and suffering (Jones 2003: 77). For the founder of Buddhism, the major way of transcending suffering is via meditative techniques which suspend language and the symbolic. Of course, in later stages, as in most religious traditions, we have the proliferation of different types of Buddhism, the development of a variety of schools tackling philosophical and epistemological issues: for example, the nature of social reality; the void or emptiness which underlies it; the way to achieve "true" knowledge etc. And, of course, in the non-elite, popular Buddhist religiosity one finds a shift from a meditative anti-metaphysical spirituality to an attachment to dogmas, rituals, magical practices, etc. (for the distinction between elite and popular Buddhism, see Jones 2003: 63ff).

Among the great variety of Buddhist traditions it is Zen Buddhism (in most of its forms) which emphasizes types of meditation aiming at the suspension of language and thinking. From a Zen perspective, the state of enlightenment is preceded by two stages: an initial stage of the "infant's innocence" and a subsequent state which is marked by the "contamination" of human existence by language; this contamination leads to constant craving and alienation. The distinguished Zen scholar Suzuki (1949) has argued that "the basic idea of Zen is to come in touch with the inner workings of one's being and to do this in the most *direct* way possible" (my emphasis); "direct" in the above quotation means without the mediation of language. Zen Master Seung Sahn has put it more explicitly: "Zen teaching simply means not attaching to language" (1997: 244). This lack of symbolic mediation is not that of the infant. It is that of an enlightened subject who has achieved via meditation an "internal silence", an inner space where words, sentences and language in general are absent or peripheralised. It is this state of affairs that one could call *postsymbolic spirituality*. It entails the reduction or even the elimination of suffering. When psychic pain is dealt with in a rationalistic manner its powers are usually enhanced. When reasoning/thinking is suspended the subject comes in touch with painful feelings/suffering without the mediation of language. It is in this manner that wordless contact with pain alleviates pain and decreases alienation and estrangement.

Conclusion

The aim of this paper is not to deny the importance, both theoretical and therapeutic, of Lacanian theory and psychoanalytic practice. It merely suggests that since Lacan's main focus was on language and speech (1966: 144-208), Lacanians should explore more systematically cases where language is suspended or bracketed. When this bracketing is successful, it tends to lead to states (more or less lasting) where the subject feels less divided, less alienated, more open and compassionate towards the self and the other. This suspension of language and thinking can be achieved by meditative methods which do not necessarily require a religious background. In cases of both believers and non- believers we observe via meditation the emergence of a type of spirituality, religious or secular, which Lacanian psychoanalysis should take more seriously into account.

The paper also suggests that one way of articulating the spiritual with Lacanian theory is via the notions of the real and of jouissance. From the total undifferentiated jouissance of the pre-symbolic period to the partial jouissance of the symbolic regime, the suspension of language may lead to a postsymbolic jouissance of a spiritual kind. The latter is not exactly the "other jouissance" of the mystic that Lacan refers to. In what one can call "meditational jouissance" the subject's basic, constitutive division does not of course disappear. But her/his sense of alienation can be considerably attenuated. To put it differently, the bracketing of language and the symbolic via meditation leads to an articulation of the symbolic with the non-symbolic, of thinking with non-thinking, which reduces considerably the subject's never-ending lack that Lacan has put at the centre of his analysis.

Appendix II

Decision Making and the Meditative Subject:
A Fourfold Typology

The aim of this text is not to produce a full model, normative or empirically based, of how the four types of subject that I am going to deal with decide on a course of action. Instead I will focus on two analytically distinct dimensions of the decision-making process:

    i.   The Voluntaristic Dimension

        The extent to which the subject is not a passive product of psycho- or sociostructural determinations, the extent to which, within the limits imposed by various structural constraints and enablements, she/he has reasonable decision making capacities, ie she/he has enough autonomy to assess and choose between alternative courses of action.

    ii.   The Dualism-duality Dimension

        Following Giddens' conceptualisation of the distinction (1984: 25-29 and 297-304), in the case of dualism there is a clear separation between the subjective and the objective, between agency and structure; and this in the sense that the subject takes a certain distance from her/his environment of action in order to assess the most adequate means for achieving the goal chosen. In other terms, dualism entails a subject who is measuring, assessing, planning, and strategizing. In the case of duality on the other hand, the distance between subject and her/his decision-making environment is minimised or disappears[1]. As I will argue below in examining Bourdieu's dispositional subject, the complex process of assessing, calculating, strategizing is in most cases minimised since the subject's habitus leads more or less automatically to the appropriate action outcome.

On the basis of the voluntaristic and the dualism/duality dimensions, I propose the following schema:

---

[1] For a critique of Giddens' distinction, see Mouzelis 1991.

	strong voluntarism	weak voluntarism
dualism	rational-choice subject	passive subject
duality	meditative/apophatic subject	dispositional/habitus subject

The Rational-Choice Subject: Dualism and Strong Voluntarism

In the huge literature on decision making, normative theories (Marxist[2] and non-Marxist[3]) focus on the means that the subject should choose in order to achieve a chosen goal in the most "rational" manner i.e., by following maximization or optimization criteria. Empirically oriented theories on the other hand focus on actual decision-making processes as they unfold in specific social contexts (enterprises, offices, laboratories etc.). The latter theories criticize the former by pointing out that *homo rationalis* is a fiction; that actual subjects do not decide in the manner that normative theories imply. In most cases there are serious discrepancies between the ideal typical and the actual decision-making process, the latter taking place in specific temporal and special contexts (Przeworski 1986: ch. 4). Normativists reply that their theories are qualitatively different from empirical decision-making studies. They have a different logical structure and raise different types of issues. More precisely normatively oriented rational choice theories tend to raise *counterfactual* questions such as: if we assume that actors have pre-constituted fixed characteristics (such as identities, interests, maximum rational capacities etc.), how will they react to various games or to various changes (i.e., price fluctuations) in their decision-making environment? Therefore the model's logico-deductive character helps one to formulate certain *tendencies* (e.g. that the investment rate will fall when interest rates rise). Of course, such tendencies can be neutralised or reversed by counter tendencies.

It is important to note, however, that in an attempt to make the normative rational-choice model more "realistic" there have been several attempts to introduce considerations of institutional context. In the so called "rational choice institutionalism" actors' preferences and utility maximization assumptions are still taken for granted but institutions are brought in as mechanisms which can resolve collective dilemmas: in so far as actors are often inhibited in following the most rational strategy because they are unable to predict other actors' behaviour, institutions provide the rational decision-maker with useful information about likely reactions of others. Institutions therefore stabilise, render more predictable the decision-maker's social environment (Hall & Taylor 1994 and 1998, Hollingsworth et al. 2002). Another element which rational-choice institutionalists introduce is the idea that strategic interaction, a notion which occupies centre stage in their approach, is partly structured by institutions. Actors still have fixed preferences, but the strategic calculations which are necessary for achieving their

---

[2] See, for instance, Cohen 1978, Elster 1985 and Roemer 1986.
[3] See, for instance, Popkin 1979, Boudon 1987 and Coleman 1990.

preferred goals are not given in advance, they are shaped by the institutional context within which they interact[4].

For our purposes, as far as the *dualism/duality* dimension is concerned, both normative and empirically oriented studies are characterised by dualism. The same is true about the rational-choice institutionalism approach which has tried to bring the two previous approaches closer together. The subject always takes distance from her/his environment in order to gather information about the conditions and means relevant to goal achievement, about the pros and cons of various strategies etc. In contrast, as I will argue below, such a distance disappears in the duality case.

As to the *voluntaristic* dimension, the rational-choice subject is conceived neither as a passive product of sociocultural determinations[5] nor as being driven by unconscious forces or compulsive drives. Within the context of existing structural constraints and enablements s/he is capable to exercise her/his decision-making capacities. In the normative, ideal typical model such capabilities are considered fully developed. In the empirically oriented model the effectiveness of such capabilities vary from case to case but they are never absent.

The Passive Subject: Dualism and Weak Voluntarism

The most representative theory of weak voluntarism or subject passivity is to be found in Talcott Parsons' work. Among the innumerable criticisms of Parsonian theory, probably the most well-known is that he conceptualises actors (particularly in the *social system* phase of his work) as "cultural dopes", as passive products of institutional, systemic determinations. Contrary however to early, rather superficial critiques of Parsonian structural functionalism, this passivity does not mean that the Parsonian subject simply follows her/his role's normative requirements. For Parsonian actors may or may not follow such requirements without this necessarily bringing "corrective", equilibrating mechanisms. The same is true about the critiques that for the American theorist common values

---

[4] Rational-choice institutionalism, by considering preferences as pre-constituted but calculations as internal to their model, occupies a position midway between conventional or "pure" rational-choice theory (where both factors are external) and an approach called "historical institutionalism" which seriously takes into account context, time- and space-wise; and which therefore considers both preferences and modes of calculation as internal. In the latter approach interests and identities are shaped, reproduced and transformed by actors who interact within historically evolving institutional contexts. Needless to say, historical institutionalism, which developed as a reaction to rational-choice theory's neglect of institutional context, does not differ much from historical sociology, or, for that matter, from conventional sociological analysis. Another way of putting this is to argue that the more rational-choice institutionalists come close to historical institutionalism let's say by considering information or modes of calculation as not given in advance the more their generalizations lose their deductive rigour; the more they portray the "messy", context-sensitive character of general sociological generalizations. For an exposition of historical institutionalism, see Thelen and Steinmo 1992. For a debate between critics and defenders of the approach, see Hall and Taylor 1998 and Hay and Wincott 1998.

[5] See next section on the Parsonian passive subject.

integrate the societal system in such a way that social order, harmony and stable equilibrium is always achieved. Contrary to the above critiques, for Parsons in any specific social system (community, formal organization, nation state etc.) the degree of system integration or social order is an empirical question. In certain cases it is high; in other cases it can be low or non-existent. In other terms, Parsonian theory allows for disorder, chaos, system disintegration. (Mouzelis 2008: 9-12)

In view of the above I would argue that the passivity/weak voluntarism of the Parsonian subject has to do with the fact that Parsons tends to show how systems and subsystems influence (without determining) actors' practice but not how the latter reproduce and transform these systems.

Let me make the above more concrete by taking as an example the Parsonian conceptualisation of the relationship between the cultural, the social and the personality systems. The cultural system refers to general values which, as we move from the cultural to the social system, these values are *institutionalised*. They take the form of roles and their normative requirements; as well as role complexes or institutions which in turn constitute the social system's four basic subsystems: economic/adaptation, political/goal achievement, social/integration and cultural/latency. Finally as one moves from the social to the personality system values and norms are *internalised* taking the form of needs/dispositions.

What is striking in the above conceptualisation is that the movement from the cultural to the social and from the social to the personality system is a *one-way process*. The focus is on how values, norms, needs/dispositions influence actors never how the latter construct or transform the former. The values, as the starting point of analysis seem to hang in the air so to speak. The historical struggles between actors which explain why certain values prevail in a social system are ignored. In other terms, the direction of influence is from the system to the actor, never the other way around.

And one sees a similar one-way treatment as far as social roles are concerned. In Parsonian theory roles, as already mentioned, do not determine social action. Nor do they always lead to social conformity, harmony and system equilibrium. But Parsons does not show how actors *handle* dynamically and interactively their roles. As interpretative microsociologies have shown, the problem is less to find out whether actors follow or not the normative requirements that their roles entail and more how they use norms in the complex games in which they are involved. The crucial difference here is between finding out what the rules of a game are and whether the players follow these rules or not (the empirically oriented Parsonian approach); and focusing on how actual games are played (the interpretative microsociological approach). In the latter case actors are not shown as products but as creating or reproducing roles/institutions. For the dynamic handling of role requirements by actors participating in an ongoing game brings to the fore their agentic powers. It shows how actors constitute, reproduce and often transform normative requirements or a game's rules.

Finally, a similar passivity one detects when we move from the social to the personality system, from roles/norms to their internalisation as needs/dispositions. On that level actor's "internal conversations", the dynamic of self-self *intra*-action which is directly linked to self-other interaction is also missing. Needs/dispositions surely influence social action. But so do the ways in which needs/dispositions are activated by actors in specific contexts, in their everyday dealings. For instance, what is missing in the Parsonian analysis on this point is what ethnomethodologists call "internal reporting". The fact that as actors interact with other actors in specific encounters there is a continuous flow of self-self-internal conversations as each actor assesses the other's reaction before making her/his move. To conclude, whether Parsons refers to the cultural system's general values, to the social system's roles or to the personality system's needs/dispositions the direction of influence is from the system to the actors, never from actors to systems.

Moving now to the decision-making process, in terms of voluntarism, the passivity that characterises the Parsonian subject in general is also a feature of the Parsonian decision maker. And this in the sense that the conceptual tools offered help us to see how the cultural, social, personality systems influence the decision-making process but not the opposite; i.e., how actor's decisions have an impact on sociocultural and personality systems in general and on the actor's decision making environment in particular. As a result Parsonian theory underemphasises the dynamic, intra- and interactive dimensions of the decision making process.

For Parsons the subject's decision-making environment consists of *conditions* and *means*. The former are, from the point of view of the decision maker, "givens", they cannot be changed by her/him. The latter entail choice. The subject can choose between different means to achieve a specific goal. As to the manner by which goals are chosen, Parsons rejects economistic and utilitarian approaches. He emphasizes the crucial role that values, norms and needs/dispositions play in the process of choice. The same is true about the choice of means. Cultural and normative rather than maximization or optimization criteria are emphasized[6]. However the shift from the neo-classical economic logic to a more sociocultural logic does not affect the system→actor, one way approach. It is clearly an approach entailing *weak voluntarism*.

As to the *duality-dualism* dimension, it is clear that Parsons' work, following the conventional distinction between actor and social structure, entails *dualism*. The decision maker takes a distance from the decision-making environment in order, following cultural/normative criteria, to choose a goal, as well as to gather information about means before deciding on how to achieve the chosen goal. And given the Parsonian emphasis on the social structure→actor rather than the actor→social structure perspective, the distance between decision maker and her/his environment of action is enhanced — since the latter perspective is underemphasized or entirely missing.

---

[6] For the Parsonian means-end schema, see Parsons 1937: 44ff.

The Dispositional/Habitus Subject: Duality and Weak Voluntarism

The focus here will be on Bourdieu's theory of practice. Bourdieu's famous *habitus* concept refers to a set of dispositions consisting of generative schemata of cognition, perception, evaluation etc. Actors acquire such schemata in the course of their socialization. They enable them to relate skilfully to others in varied social contexts. The French theorist sees the habitus as entailing an *objective* dimension, since it is based on the internalization of historically evolved and evolving objective social structures. It also entails a *subjective* dimension since it is the means of relating to others, of participating in the games of everyday life (1990). Therefore in order to understand a social practice one must examine how social structures, via processes of socialisation, become dispositions which lead to social practices. In turn, such practices reproduce social structures. Therefore schematically we have:

$$S \text{ (Social Structure)} \rightarrow D \text{ (Dispositions)} \rightarrow P \text{ (Practices)}$$

Concerning the voluntaristic dimension, the SDP scheme has often been critisized as being deterministic/mechanistic (Jenkins 1991). Bourdieu has defended his position by arguing that the habitus concept does not automatically lead to practices; on the contrary, the set of dispositions that constitute the habitus have a flexible, polysemic and polythetic character. Rather than strictly determining practices they operate as a limiting framework within which different practices are produced. "The habitus, like every 'act of inventing', is what makes possible to produce an infinite number of practices that are relatively unpredictable, even if they are limited in their diversity" (1990: 63). For Bourdieu it is the inventive flexibility that allows the habitus carrier, when s/he enters a specific field, to cope with the field's varied requirements that positions entail. He stresses however that "polythetic adaptability" operates in a *taken for granted, non-reflexive* manner. Hence Bourdieu provides no conceptual tools sensitising the student to processes of strategying, of planning, of choosing between alternatives. In "normal" circumstances the habitus operates in a way which entails neither calculation nor elaborate decision making; it operates in a way that an actor's dispositions and the field's positions lead to practices without activation of rationally based choices. It is only in crisis situations, when there are discrepancies between dispositions and positions, that reflexivity and rational decision making are activated (Bourdieu & Wacquant 1992: 131).

It may be argued that it is unfair to criticize Bourdieu's overall theory for lack of voluntarism. It could be argued that unlike Parsons, Bourdieu constantly refers to actors' struggles, to their strategies aimed at the acquisition of a field's economic, political and symbolic capital. But neither the struggles nor the strategies in his theory entail rational calculation of conditions, or reflexive handling of the means to be used in order to achieve specific goals. Strategies are generated and unfold in a taken-for-granted, quasi-automatic manner, as actors mobilise their dispositional potential within a field's interrelated set of positions.

Therefore in "normal" conditions rational, calculating, voluntaristic elements of decision-making are absent or peripheral: "The most profitable strategies are usually those produced, *without any calculation*, and in the most absolute "sincerity", by a habitus objectively fitted to the objective structures. These *strategies without strategic calculations* produce an important secondary advantage for those who *can scarcely be called their authors*: the social approval occurring to apparent disinterestedness" (Bourdieu 1990: 292, emphasis added).

One can of course argue that the concept of strategy always entails conscious calculation. But irrespective of Bourdieu's idiosyncratic use of the term, there is no doubt that the voluntaristic elements in his theory are rather weak. From a comparative perspective however, Bourdieu's subject is more voluntaristic rather than Parsons' "oversocialised" one. Bourdieu's conceptualisation of the subject entails, at least in exceptional cases (i.e., where there is a clash between dispositions and positions) a type of reflexivity which implies not only the social structure→actor dimension but also the actor→social structure one.

But despite this, as already mentioned, Bourdieu sees social practices as the outcome of the positional (field) as well as the dispositional (habitus) dimensions of social games. What is missing is the interactive-situational dimension. Practices in actual social games cannot be fully explained in terms of positions and dispositions. A satisfactory explanation must also take into account the more voluntaristic strategying dimension; the fact that actors, in varying degrees, take seriously into account the practices/reactions of others actors involved in the same game. This necessarily indicates a type of strategying which is qualitatively different from Bourdieu's "strategies without calculation" (Mouzelis 2008: 119-121). To conclude, Bourdieu's conceptualisation of the subject, to a lesser extent than in Parsonian theory, is clearly a case of *weak voluntarism*.

If Bourdieu's decision-making subject can be characterised as entailing weak voluntarism, on the dualism-duality dimension he stresses subject-object *duality* rather than dualism. The subjective-objective divide is not abolished but transcended via a "structurationist" approach [7] which regards the habitus as entailing both the "subjective" (habitus as 'structuring structures') and the "objective" (habitus as the product of structures). To put it in terms of our conceptualisation, the subject relates to the environment of action (object) in such a manner that there is no distance between the two. The decision maker need not take distance from the means of action in order to calculate and assess the different, possible courses leading to the goal. The strategying process is peripheralised or completely eliminated. It is in this way that the conventional distinction between agency and structure, decision maker and decisional environment is transcended.

---

[7] For a critical analysis of the structurationist approach, see Parker 2000. See also Archer 1982 and Mouzelis 1991: 25-47.

The Meditative/Apophatic Subject: Duality and Strong Voluntarism

Apophatic in Greek means negatory. Apophatism has played a very central role in Christian eastern orthodox theology. As mentioned in Chapter V, it entails two types of negation. The first is the idea that God is unknowable. Therefore any attempt to define his powers positively, i.e., *cataphatically*, is impossible. As in some forms of western negative theology, the believer can apophatically state what God is not, never what he is. In its *essence* the divine is beyond human comprehension. However in terms of his *energies* God is approachable in an apophatic manner — i.e. by eliminating not only passions but also and mainly thoughts and images. This process leads to "emptying" the soul of all ruminations, calculations, rationalising elements. When this is achieved the soul becomes an "empty vessel" ready to receive divine grace, God's energies. As to the way to achieve this, i.e., to stop or peripheralise cognitive processes, this is via various types of discipline such as correct posture and breathing, silent contemplation, repetition of a short prayer, concentration on an icon or other sacred objects etc. (Mouzelis 2010).

Of course both forms of negation (unkownability of God and emptying) are to be found in most religious/mystical traditions east and west, Christian and non-Christian[8]. In late modernity however the emptying process has taken secular forms; in the sense that meditative techniques aiming at the cessation or rather momentary peripheralisation of cognitive processes are not necessarily linked to a religious tradition. Particularly in the western world, informal meditation networks or centres (which may or may not be linked to a church) are spreading rapidly; especially among the educated middle classes[9]. Even hospitals, particularly in the United States, use meditation as a means of reducing anxiety and enhancing a sense of well-being among patients, patients who may be believers, non-believers or agnostics. There is in other terms a "downwards" movement from a restricted number of religious, spiritual elites (mystics, ascetics, monks etc.) to believers and non-believers at the non-elite level. To put it differently, the premodern chasm between elite and non-elite popular religiosity or spirituality is narrowing (Sharot 2001).

It is in the above sense that one can talk about an apophatic decision-making subject. A subject who reaches decisions in a negatory manner. Decisions in this case are not reached by following the conventional rational choice mode. There is neither a conscious choice of goals, nor a systematic gathering of information and rational assessment of the most adequate means for achieving a goal. Decisions in

---

[8] Buddhism (particularly Zen Buddhism) in its non-popular, elite spirituality is probably the religion which stresses more meditative techniques aiming at the suspension of thinking and less on metaphysical doctrines on the nature of the divine, what happens after death etc. Thus the historical Buddha was refusing to answer his disciples' metaphysical questions. He was constantly reminding them that his aim was not to teach about the existence or non-existence of God but how to overcome, via meditation, human suffering (Jones 2003: 77).
[9] See on this point Heelas and Woodhead 2005, Roof 2001 and Mouzelis 2012.

other terms are predominately not the result of rational thinking. Rather they *emerge* spontaneously via the suspension of thinking, via the creation of an internal space where pondering alternative courses of action, planning, calculating, strategying etc. are absent or peripheral. Within this empty space divine energies from above (in the case of believers), or untapped human potentialities from within, lead to crucial decisions without rationalising processes. One knows spontaneously what to do, how to relate to the other, what course of action to take without any calculation or planning.

As far as the two dimensions of our problematic are concerned, we have strong *voluntarism and duality*. Concerning the former, the subject portrays a "negative" type of strong voluntarism. In an autonomous but apophatic manner s/he chooses not to do but to undo, not to construct but to deconstruct, not to think but to create internal emptiness or void. If language and the "symbolic" in Lacanian theory lead to the "barred" or divided subject, the apophatic subject creates a space within which language and thinking are bracketed. It is such a state that the mystic tries to achieve in an effort to approach or even unite with the divine (theosis). It is a similar thought/language bracketing that those practicing meditation (believers and non-believers) try to achieve even for a short period of time. They try to achieve internal silence and to overcome the "tyranny" of rational decision-making in a late modern context where choices are multiplied in geometric fashion.

As to the duality-dualism dimension, here duality prevails. The distance between the apophatic subject and her/his environment does not exist. Thus the dualism between decision maker and her/his environment of action disappears. The apophatic subject chooses neither means nor goals. Decisions on the choice of goals and means are not cognitively achieved; they emerge without rational choice processes.

Conclusion

The four types of subject discussed above constitute, of course, ideal types. In actual situations of problem-solving elements of several or all of them are present. To put it differently, the rational/voluntaristic, the passive/less voluntaristic, the dispositional and the meditative/apophatic are, in most cases, present when actors try to organise their everyday existence. Of course in specific contexts and according to the problem requiring solution, one of the four logics is dominant. If the gaol is, for instance, to repair a machine, the engineer will operate mainly but not exclusively on the basis of the rational-choice/voluntaristic mode. On the other hand, in more traditional contexts (as those studied by Bourdieu in his Algerian fieldwork)[10] reflexivity, rational planning and strategizing is peripheralised. The subject's habitus leads her/him to opt in a quasi-automatic manner for a certain

---

[10] For an overview of Bourdieu's work on Algeria, see Robbins 1991: 10-28.

course of action which is traditionally legitimised. As to the case of the passive/weak voluntaristic logic, this becomes dominant in social contexts where structural constraints, without determining, limit severely alternative sources of action. Finally, the apophatic mode of letting decisions emerge spontaneously can be dominant in the sphere of intimate interpersonal relations.

References

Ahmad, A.A. (1975). *A History of Islamic Sicily*. Edinburgh: Edinburgh University Press.
Alexander, J.C. (1998). *Neo-Functionalism and After: Collected Readings*. Oxford: Blackwell.
Alexander, J.C. (2003). *The Meanings of Social Life: A Cultural Sociology*. Oxford: Oxford University Press.
Alvesson, M., and K. Sköldberg (2000). *Reflexive Methodology: New Vistas for Qualitative Research*. London: Sage.
Ammerman, N.T. (1994). "The Dynamics of Christian Fundamentalism: An Introduction" in M.E. Marty and R.S. Appleby (eds). *Accounting for Fundamentalism: The Dynamic Character of Movements*. Chicago: University of Chicago Press, pp. 13-17.
Anderson, B. (1991). *Imagined Communities: Reflections on the Origin and Spread of Nationalism*. London: Verso.
Anderson, P. (1974).*Lineages of the Absolutist State*. London: New Left Publications.
Archer, M.S. (1982). "Morphogenics versus Structuration: On Combining Structure and Agency", *British Journal of Sociology*, Vol. 33, No. 4, pp. 455-483.
Archer, M. (2003). *Structure, Agency and the Internal Conversation*. Cambridge: Cambridge University Press.
Armstrong, K. (2006). *The Great Transformation: The World in the Time of Buddha, Socrates, Confucius and Jeremiah*. London: Atlantic Books.
Arjomand, S.A. (1988). *The Turban for the Crown: The Islamic Revolution in Iran*. New York: Oxford University Press.
Attwater, D. (1965). *The Penguin Dictionary of Saints*. London: Penguin Books.
Bakhash, S. (1984). *The Region of the Ayatollahs: Iran and the Islamic Revolution*. New York: Basic Books.
Bauman, Z. (1987). *Legislators and Interpreters: On Modernity, Postmodernity and Intellectuals*. Ithaca: Cornell University Press.
Bauman, Z. (1992). *Intimations of Postmodernity*. New York: Routledge.
Bauman, Z. (1993). *Postmodern Ethics*. Oxford: Blackwell.
Beck, U. (1992). *Risk Society: Towards a new modernity*. London: Sage.
Beck, U. (2000). *The Brave New World of Work*. Cambridge: Polity Press.
Beck, U. (2010). *A God of One's Own: Religion's Capacity for Peace and Potential for Violence*. Cambridge: Polity Press.
Beck, U., and E. Beck-Gernsheim (2003). *Individualization: Institutionalized Individualism and its Social and Political Consequences*. London: Sage.
Beck, U., and C. Lau (2005). "Second Modernity as a Research Agenda: Theoretical and Empirical Exploration in the 'Meta-Change' of Modern Society", *British Journal of Sociology*, Vol. 56, No 4, pp. 525-557.
Beckford, J., A., and T. Luckman (eds) (1989). *The Changing Face of Religion*. London: Sage.
Bedford-Strohm, H. and C. Deane-Drummond (eds) (2011). *Religion and Ecology in the Public Sphere*. London: Continuum.
Bernard, C., and K. Zalmay (1984). *The Government of God: Iran's Islamic Republic*. New York: Columbia University Press.
Beyer, P. (1994). *Religion and Globalisation*. London: Sage.
Bharier, J. (1971). *Economic Development in Iran, 1900-1970*. London: Oxford University Press.
Billig, M. (1995). *Banal Nationalism*. London: Sage.
Borne, E. (1961). *Atheism*. New York: Hawthorn Books.
Boudon, R. (1987). "The Individualistic Tradition in Sociology" in J. Alexander, B. Giesen, R. Münch and N. Smelser (eds). *The Micro-Macro Link*. California: University of California Press, pp. 45-70.
Bourdieu, P. (1990). *The Logic of Practice*. Cambridge: Polity Press.
Bourdieu, P. (2004). *Science of Science and Reflexivity*. Chicago: University of Chicago Press.
Bourdieu, P., and L. Wacquant (1992). *An Invitation to Reflexive Sociology*. Cambridge: Polity Press.

Bracher, M. (1997). "Editor's Column: Psychoanalysis and Racism", *Journal for the Psychoanalysis of Culture and Society*, Vol. 2, No. 2, pp. 1-11.
Bruce, S. (1988). *Fundamentalism*. Cambridge: Polity Press.
Bruce, S. (2011). *Secularization: In Defence of an Unfashionable Theory*. Oxford: Oxford University Press.
Buber, M. (1937). *I and Thou*. Edinburgh: T. and T. Clark.
Buber, M. (1947). *Between Man and Man*. London: Routledge.
Buber, M. (1952). *Eclipse of God: Studies in the Relation between Religion and Philosophy*. New York: Harper.
Buber, M. (1967). "Replies to my Critics" in P.A. Schilp and M. Friedman (eds). *The Philosophy of Martin Buber*. La Salle, Illinois: Open Court, pp. 692-693.
Calvert, J. (2010). *Sayyid Qutb and the Origins of Radical Islamism*. New York: Columbia University Press.
Carnegie, D. (1938). *How to Win Friends and Influence People*. New York: Simon and Schuster.
Carrete, J. and R. King (2005). *Selling Spirituality: The Silent Takeover of Religion*. London: Routledge.
Castells, M. (1996). *The Rise of the Network Society. Vol. I. The. Information Age: Economy, Society, and Culture*. Oxford: Blackwell.
Chaitin, G. (1996). *Rhetoric and Culture in Lacan*. Cambridge: Cambridge University Press.
Clark, G. (1969). "The Social Foundation of States" in F.L. Carsten, (ed.). *The New Cambridge Modern History. Vol. 5: The Ascendancy of France 1648–88*. Cambridge: Cambridge University Press.
Clarke, S., and J. Bird (1999). "Racism, Hatred and Discrimination through the Lens of Projective Identification", *Journal for the Psychoanalysis of Culture and Society*, Vol. 4, No. 2, pp. 158-161.
Cohen, G.A. (1978). *Karl Marx's Theory of History: A Defence*. Oxford: Clarendon Press.
Coleman, J.S. (1990). *Foundations of Social Theory*. Cambridge: The Belknap Press of Harvard University Press.
Comte, A. (1976). *The Foundations of Sociology*. London: Nelson.
Coward, H., and T. Foshay (eds) (1992). *Derrida and Negative Theology*. Albany: State University of New York Press.
Crook, S, J. Pakulski and M. Waters (1992). *Postmodernization: Change in Advanced Society*. London: Sage.
Cupitt, D. (1980). *Taking Leave of God*. London: SCM Press.
Cupitt, D. (1984). *The Sea of Faith*. Cambridge: Cambridge University Press.
Davie, G. (1994). *Religion in Britain since 1945*. Oxford: Blackwell.
Dawkins, R. (2007). *The God Delusion*. London: Transworld Publishers.
Dennet, D. (2006). *Breaking the Spell: Religion as a Natural Phenomenon*. London: Allen Lane.
Diamond, L., and M. Plattner (eds) (1996). *The Global Resurgence of Democracy*. Baltimore: John Hopkins University Press.
Dobb, M. (1968). *Studies in the Development of Capitalism*. New York: International Publishers.
Douglas, M., and S. Tipton (1983). *Religion and America: Spirituality in a Secular Age*. Boston: Beacon Press.
Douzinas, C. (2000). *The End of Human Rights: Critical Legal Thought at the Turn of the Century*. Oxford: Hart Publishing.
Eisenstadt, S.N. (1963). *The Political Systems of Empires*. New York: Free Press.
Eisenstandt, S.N. (1999). *Fundamentalism, Sectarianism and Revolution: The Jacobin Dimensions of Modernity*. Cambridge: Cambridge University Press.
Elias, N. (1982). *The Civilizing Process: The History of Manners*. Oxford: Blackwell.
Elias, N. (1991). *The Society of Individuals*. Oxford: Blackwell.
Elliot, P. (1996). "Working Through Racism: Confronting the Strangely Familiar", *Journal for the Psychoanalysis of Culture and Society*, Vol. 1, No. 1, pp. 63-72.
Ellis, C., and A. Bochner (2000). "Autoethnography, Personal Narrative, Reflexivity: Researcher as Subject" in N. Denzin and Y. Lincoln (eds). *Handbook of Qualitative Research*. Thousand Oaks: Sage, pp. 733-768.
Elster, J. (1985). *Making Sense of Marx*. Cambridge: Cambridge University Press.

References

Epstein, M. (1999). "Post-Atheism: From Apophatic Theology to 'Minimal Religion'" in M. Epstein, A. Genis and S. Vladiv-Glover (eds). *Russian Postmodernism: New Perspectives on Post-Soviet Culture*. New York: Berghahn Books, pp. 431-479.
Evdokimov, P. (1965). *L' Orthodoxie*. Neuchâtel: Delachaux et Niestlé.
Ferguson, W.S. (1969). "The Leading Ideas of the New Period" in J.B. Bury, S.A. Cook and F.E. Adcock (eds). *The Cambridge Ancient History. Vol. VII: The Hellenistic Monarchies and the Rise of Rome*. Cambridge: Cambridge University Press.
Feuerbach, L. (1855 [1957]). *The Essence of Christianity*. New York: Harper and Row.
Fink, B. (1996). *The Lacanian Subject: Between Language and Jouissance*. Princeton: Princeton University Press.
Fink, B. (1997). *A Clinical Introduction to Lacanian Psychoanalysis: Theory and Technique*. Cambridge: Harvard University Press.
Fox, M. (1967). "Some Problems in Buber's Moral Philosophy" in P.A. Schilpp and M. Friedman (eds). *The Philosophy of Martin Buber*. La Salle, Illinois: Open Court, pp. 151-170.
Frazer, E., and N. Lacey (1994). "MacIntyre, Feminism and the Concept of Practice" in J. Horton and S. Mendus (eds). *After MacIntyre: Critical Perspectives on the work of Alasdair MacIntyre*. Cambridge: Polity Press, pp. 265-282.
Friedman, M. (1955). *Martin Buber: The Life of Dialogue*. London: Routledge and Kegan Paul.
Fukuyama, F. (1992). *The End of History and the Last Man*. New York: Free Press.
Fuller, R.C. (2001). *Spiritual but not Religious: Understanding Unchurched America*. Oxford: Oxford University Press.
Gellner, E. (1969). *Saints of the Atlas*. London: Weidenfeld and Nicolson.
Gellner, E. (1981). *Muslim Society*. Cambridge: Cambridge University Press.
Giddens, A. (1984). *The Constitution of Society: Outline of the Theory of Structuration*. Cambridge: Polity Press.
Giddens, A. (1985). *A Contemporary Critique of Historic Materialism. Vol. 2: The Nation State and Violence*. London: Macmillan.
Giddens, A. (1990). *The Consequences of Modernity*. Cambridge: Polity Press.
Giddens, A. (1994). "Living in a Post-Traditional Society". In U. Beck, A. Giddens and S. Lash (eds). *Reflexive Modernisation: Politics, Tradition and Aesthetics in the Modern Social Order*. Cambridge: Polity Press, pp. 54-109.
Glock, C.Y. and R. Bellah (eds) (1976). *The New Religious Consciousness*. Berkeley: University of California Press.
Gouldner, A. (1971). *The Coming Crisis of Western Sociology*. London: Heinemann.
Graham, R. (1979). *Iran: The Illusion of Power*. London: Croom Helm.
Habermas, J. (1984). *The Theory of Communicative Action. Vol. 1: Reason and the Rationalization of Society*. London: Heinemann.
Habermas, J. (1987). *The Theory of Communicative Action. Vol. 2: Lifeworld and System: A Critique of Functional Reason*. London: Heinemann.
Hall, A.P. and R.C.R. Taylor (1994). "Political Science and the Four Institutionalisms", *Annual Meeting of the American Political Science Association*, New York.
Hall, A.P. and R.C.R. Taylor (1998). "The Potential of Historical Institutionalism: A Response to Hay and Wincott", *Political Studies*, Vol. 46, No. 5, pp. 958-962.
Hall, S. and B. Grieben (eds) (1992). *The Formations of Modernity: Understanding Modern Societies*. Cambridge: Polity Press.
Halliday, F. (1994). "The Politics of Islamic Fundamentalism: Iran, Tunisia and the Challenge to the Secular State" in A.S. Ahmed and H. Donnan (eds). *Islam, Globalization and Postmodernity*. London: Routledge, pp. 91-113.
Hampton, K.N. and B. Wellman (2002). "The not so Global Village of Neville" in B. Wellman and C. Haythornthwaite (eds). *The Internet in Everyday Life*. Oxford: Blackwell, pp. 345-371.
Harmless, W. (2008). *Mystics*. Oxford: Oxford University Press.
Harris, S. (2005). *The End of Faith: Religion, Terror, and the Future of Reason*. London: Free Press.
Hay, C. and D. Wincott (1998). "Structure, Agency and Historical Institutionalism", *Political Studies*, Vol. 46, No. 5, pp. 951-957.
Heelas, P. (2008). *Spiritualities of Life: New Age Romanticism and Consumptive Capitalism*. Oxford: Blackwell.

Heelas, P. and L. Woodhead (2005). *The Spiritual Revolution: Why Religion is Giving Way to Spirituality*. Oxford: Blackwell.
Heelas P., S. Lash and P. Morris (eds) (1996). *Detraditionalization*. Cambridge: Blackwell.
Heidegger, M. (1974). "The Principle of Ground", *Man and World*, Vol. 7, No. 3, pp. 207-222.
Herrick, J.A. (2003). *The Making of the New Spirituality: The Eclipse of the Western Religious Tradition*. Downers Grove, Illinois: InterVarsity Press.
Hick, J. (1989). *An Interpretation of Religion: Human Responses to the Transcendent*. London: Macmillan Press.
Hirschman, A. (1970). *A Bias for Hope Essays: On Development and Latin America*. New Haven: Yale University Press.
Hobsbawm, E. (1968). *Industry and Empire: The Birth of the Industrial Revolution*. London: Penguin.
Hollingsworth, J.R., K.H. Muller and E.J. Hollingsworth (2002). *Advancing Socioeconomics: An Institutionalist Perspective*. Lanham, Maryland: Rowman and Littlefield.
Holroyd. S. (1980). *The Quest of the Quiet Mind: The Philosophy of Krishnamurti*. Wellingborough, Northamptonshire: The Aquarian Press.
Hoogvelt, A.M. (1978). *The Sociology of Developing Societies*. London: Macmillan.
Ishay, M.R. (2004). "What Are Human Rights? Six Historical Controversies", *Journal of Human Rights*, Vol. 3, No. 3, pp. 359-371.
James, W. (1902 [1977]). *The Varieties of Religious Experience: A Study in Human Nature*. London: Fontana Books.
Jaspers, K. (1953). *The Origin and Goal of History*. London: Routledge and Kegan Paul.
Jenkins, R. (1991). *Pierre Bourdieu*. London: Routledge.
Jones, J.W. (2003). *The Mirror of God: Christian Faith as Spiritual Practice: Lessons from Buddhism and Psychoanalysis*. New York: Palgrave Macmillan.
Jung, H.Y. (1990). "Heidegger's Way with Sinitic Thinking" in G. Parkes (ed.). *Heidegger and Asian Thought*. Honolulu: University of Hawaii Press.
King, U. (1998). *Christian Mystics: The Spiritual Heart of the Christian Tradition*. New York: Simon and Schuster.
Klein, M. (1946). "Notes on Some Schizoid Mechanisms", *International Journal of Psychoanalysis*, No. 27, pp. 99-110.
Kramer, K. (1986). *World Scriptures: An Introduction to Comparative Religions*. New York: Paulist Press.
Krishnamurti, J. (1954). *The First and Last Freedom*. London: Gollancz.
Krishnamurti, J. (1956). *Commentaries on Living*. London: Gollancz.
Krishnamurti, J. (1969). *Freedom from the Known*. London: Gollancz.
Krishnamurti, J. (1972). *The Impossible Question*. London: Gollancz.
Krishnamurti, J. (1975). *Beginnings of Learning*. London: Gollancz.
Krishnamurti, J. (1978). *The Wholeness of Life*. London: Gollancz.
Krishnamurti, J. (1985). *The Ending of Time*. London: Gollancz.
Kotoh, T. (1990). "Language and Silence: Self-Inquiry in Heidegger and Asian Thought" in G. Parkes (ed.). *Heidegger and Asian Thought*. Honolulu: University of Hawaii Press.
Lacan, J. (1966). *Ecrits I*. Paris: Seuil.
Lacan, J. (1975). *Livre XX: Encore*. Paris: Seuil.
Lacan, J. (1977). *The Four Fundamental Concepts of Psycho-Analysis*. London: The Hogarth Press.
Lawson, H. (1985). *Reflexivity: The Post-Modern Predicament*. La Salle, Illinois: Open Court.
Levinas, E. (1967). "Martin Buber and the Theory of Knowledge" in P.A. Schilpp and M. Friedman (eds). *The Philosophy of Martin Buber*. La Salle, Illinois: Open Court, pp. 133-149.
Levinas, E. (1981). *Otherwise than Being or Beyond Essence*. The Hague: Martinus Nijhoff.
Llewelyn, J. (1995). *Emmanuel Levinas: The Genealogy of Ethics*. London: Routledge.
Lossky, V. (1944). *Essai sur la Théologie Mystique de l' Eglise d' Orient*. Aubier: Editions Montagne.
Louth, A. (2007). *The Origins of the Christian Mystical Tradition*. Oxford: Oxford University Press.
Loy, D. (1992), "The Deconstruction of Buddhism" in H. Coward and T. Forshay (eds). *Derrida and Negative Theology*. New York: State University of New York Press, pp. 227-254.
Luhmann, N. (1982). *The Differentiation of Society*. New York: Columbia University Press.
Lutyens, M. (1988). *Krishnamurti: The Open Door*. London: Murray.
Lynch, G. (2007). *The New Spirituality: An Introduction to Progressive Belief in the Twenty-First Century*. London: I.B. Tauris.

MacIntyre, A. (1988). *Whose Justice? Which Rationality?* London: Duckworth.
MacIntyre, A. (1990). *Three Rival Versions of Moral Enquiry: Encyclopaedia, Genealogy and Tradition.* Notre Dame, Indiana: Notre Dame Press.
MacIntyre, A. (2007). *After Virtue: A Study in Moral Theory.* London: Duckworth.
Mann, M. (1986). *The Sources of Social Power. Vol. 1: A History of Power from the Beginning to A.D. 1760.* Cambridge: Cambridge University Press.
Mann, M. (1992). "The Emergence of Modern European Nationalism" in J. Hall. and I. Jarvie (eds). *Transition to Modernity: Essays on Power, Wealth and Belief.* Cambridge: Cambridge University Press, pp. 137-165.
Marshall, T.H. (1964). *Class, Citizenship and Social Development.* Garden City, New York: Doubleday.
Martin, D. (2005). *On Secularization: Towards a Revised General Theory.* Aldershot, Hants: Ashgate.
Martin, D. (2011). *The Future of Christianity: Reflections on Violence and Democracy, Religion and Secularization.* Farnham, Surrey: Ashgate.
Marty, M.E., and R.S. Appleby (eds) (1994). *Fundamentalisms Observed.* Chicago: University of Chicago Press.
Marx, K. (1859 [1964]). *Pre-Capitalist Economic Formations.* London: Lawrence and Wishart.
Mauss, M. (1972). *A General Theory of Magic.* New York: Norton Library.
McCarthy, T. (1985). "Reflections on Rationalization in the Theory of Communicative Action" in R.J. Bernstein (ed.). *Habermas and Modernity.* Cambridge: Polity Press.
McNeil, W.H. (1963). *The Rise of the West: A History of the Human Community.* Chicago: University of Chicago Press.
McNeil, W. (1995). "A Swan Song for British Liberalism?" in J. Hall and I. Jarvie (eds). *The Social Philosophy of Ernest Gellner.* Amsterdam: Rodopi, pp. 565-572.
Mead, G.H. (1934). *Mind, Self and Society: From the Standpoint of a Social Behaviorist.* Chicago: University of Chicago Press.
Meyendorff, J. (1974). *St. Gregory Palamas and Orthodox Spirituality.* Crestwood, New York: St. Vladimir's Seminary Press.
Minois, G. (1998). *Histoire de l' Atheism: Les Incroyants dans Le Monde Occidental Des Origines À Nos Jours.* Paris: Arthème Fayard.
Mittelman, J.H. (2000). *The Globalization Syndrome: Transformation and Resistance.* Princeton: Princeton University Press.
Mouzelis, N. (1986). *Politics in the Semi-Periphery: Early Parliamentarism and Late Industrialisation in the Balkans and Latin America.* London: Macmillan.
Mouzelis, N. (1991). *Back to Sociological Theory: The Construction of Social Orders.* London: Macmillan.
Mouzelis, N. (1994). "The State in Late Development: Historical and Comparative Perspectives" in D. Booth (ed.). *Rethinking Social Development: Theory, Research and Practice.* Burnt Mill, Harlow: Longman, pp. 126-151.
Mouzelis, N. (1999). "Exploring Post-traditional Orders: Individual Reflexivity, 'Pure Relations' and Duality of Structure" in M. O'Brien, S. Penna and C. Hay (eds). *Theorising Modernity: Reflexivity, Environment, and Identity in Giddens' Social Theory.* London: Longman, pp. 83-97.
Mouzelis, N. (2001). "Reflexive Modernization and the Third Way: The Impasses of Giddens' Social Democratic Politics", *Sociological Review*, Vol. 49, No. 3, pp. 436-456.
Mouzelis, N. (2008). *Modern and Postmodern Social Theorising: Bridging the Divide.* Cambridge: Cambridge University Press.
Mouzelis, N. (2010). "Self And Self-Other Reflexivity: The Apophatic Dimension", *European Journal of Social Theory*, Vol. 13, No. 2, pp. 271-284.
Mouzelis, N. (2012). "Modernity and the Secularization Debate", *Sociology*, Vol. 46, No. 2, pp. 207-223.
Murdoch, I. (1996). "Who Is the Experiencer?" in *Questioning Krishnamurti: J. Krishnamurti in Dialogue.* London: Thorsons.
Qutb, S. (2000). *Social Justice in Islam.* Kuala Lumpur: Islamic Book Trust.
Parker, J. (2000). *Structuration.* Buckingham: Open University Press.
Parkes, G. (ed.) (1990). *Heidegger and Asian Thought.* Honolulu: University of Hawaii Press.
Parsons, T. (1937). *The Structure of Social Action.* New York: Free Press.

Parsons, T. (1964). "Evolutionary Universals in Society", *American Sociological Review*, Vol.29, No. 3, pp. 339-357.
Parsons, T. (1971). *The System of Modern Societies*. Englewood Cliffs, New Jersey: Prentice-Hall.
Parsons, T. (1977). *The Evolution of Societies*. Englewood Cliffs, New Jersey: Prentice Hall.
Popkin, S.L. (1979). *The Rational Peasant: The Political Economy of Rural Society in Vietnam*. Berkeley: University of California Press.
Przeworski, A. (1986). *Capitalism and Social Democracy*. Cambridge: Cambridge University Press.
Rauch, J. (2003). "Let It Be: Three Cheers for Apatheism", *The Atlantic Monthly*, May.
Rawls, J.B. (1971). *A Theory of Justice*. Oxford: Clarendon Press.
Rehm, L.P., N.J. Kaslow and A.S. Rabin (1987). "Cognitive and Behavioral Targets in a Self-Control Therapy Program for Depression", *Journal of Consulting and Clinical Psychology*, Vol. 55, No. 1, pp. 60-67.
Rinpoche, C.J. (1996). "What is Meditation" in *Questioning Krishnamurti: J. Krishnamurti in Dialogue*. London: Thorsons.
Risse, T and S. Ropp (1999). "International Human Rights norms and Domestic Change: Conclusions" in T. Risse, S. Ropp and K. Sikkink (eds). *The Power of Human Rights: International Norms and Domestic Change*. Cambridge: Cambridge University Press, pp. 234-278.
Risse, T and K. Sikkink (1999). "The Socialization of International Human Rights Norms into Domestic Practices" in T. Risse, S. Ropp and K. Sikkink (eds). *The Power of Human Rights: International Norms and Domestic Change*. Cambridge: Cambridge University Press, pp. 1-38.
Robbins, D. (1991). *The Work of Pierre Bourdieu: Recognising Society*. Milton Keynes: Open University Press.
Robbins, T. (1988). *Cults, Converts and Charisma: The Sociology of New Religious Movements*. London: Sage.
Robertson, R. (1989). 'Globalization, Politics and Religion' in J. Beckford and T. Luckmann (eds). *The Changing Face of Religion*. London: Sage, pp. 10-23.
Robertson, R. (1994). "Globalisation or Glocalisation?", *Journal of International Communication*, Vol. 1, No. 1, pp. 33-52.
Robinson, J.A.T. (1965). *The New Reformation*. London: SCM Press.
Robinson, J.A.T. (1973). *The Human Face of God*. London: SCM Press.
Roemer, J. (ed.) (1986). *Analytical Marxism*. Cambridge: Cambridge University Press.
Roof, W.C. (2001). *Spiritual Market Place: Baby Boomers and the Remaking of the American Religion*. Princeton: Princeton University Press.
Rubin, B. (2010). *The Muslim Brotherhood: The Organization and Policies of a Global Islamist Movement*. New York: Palgrave Macmillan.
Rubinstein, N. (1997). *The Government of Florence under the Medici*. Oxford: Clarendon Press.
Sachedina, A.A. (1994). "Activist Shi'ism in Iran, Iraq, and Lebanon" in M.E. Marty and R.S. Appleby (eds). *Fundamentalisms Observed*. Chicago: University of Chicago Press.
Sahlins, M.D. and E.R. Service (eds) (1960). *Evolution and Culture*. Ann Arbor: University of Michigan Press.
Sahn, S. (1997). *The Compass of Zen*. London: Shambala.
Sarroub, L. (2008). "Living 'Glocally' with Literary Success in the Midwest", *Theory into Practice*, Vol. 47, No. 1, pp. 59-66.
Schallert, E.S.J. (1996). "How Do We See That which is Most Real?" in *Questioning Krishnamurti: J. Krishnamurti in Dialogue*. London: Thorsons.
Sekida, K. (1975). *Zen Training: Methods and Philosophy*. New York: Weatherhill.
Sells, M.A. (1994). *Mystical Languages of Unsaying*. Chicago: University of Chicago Press.
Sharot, S. (2001). *A Comparative Sociology of World Religions: Virtuosos, Priests, and Popular Religion*. New York: New York University Press.
Shepherdson, C. (2008). *Lacan and the Limits of Language*. New York: Fordman University Press.
Shermer, M. (1999). *How We Believe: Science, Skepticism, and the Search for God*. New York: W.H. Freeman.
Silberstein, L. (1989). *Martin Buber's Social and Religious Thought: Alienation and the Quest for Meaning*. New York: New York University Press.
Simon, H. (1961). *Administrative Behaviour*. New York: Macmillan.

References

Sivan, E. (1985). *Radical Islam: Medieval Theology and Modern Politics*. New Haven: Yale University Press.
Sklair, Leslie (2002). *Globalization: Capitalism and Its Alternatives*. Oxford: Blackwell Publishing.
Smart, N. (1965). "Interpretation and Mystical Experience", *Religious Studies*, Vol. 1, No. 1, pp. 75-87.
Smith. S. (1983). *The Argument to the Other: Reason beyond Reason in the Thought of Karl Barth and Emmanuel Levinas*. Chico, California: Scholars Press.
Smelser, N. (1962). *Social Change in the Industrial Revolution: An Application of Theory to the Lancashire Cotton Industry 1770-1840*. London: Routledge and Kegan Paul.
Stambough, J. (1990). "Heidegger, Taoism and Metaphysics" in G. Parkes (ed.). *Heidegger and Asian Thought*. Honolulu: University of Hawaii Press.
Stavrakakis, Y. (1999). *Lacan and the Political*. London. Routledge.
Stavrakakis, Y. and N. Chrysoloras (2006). "(I Can't Get No) Enjoyment: Lacanian Theory and the Analysis of Nationalism", *Psychoanalysis, Culture and Society*, Vol. 11, No. 2, pp. 144-163.
Stein, R. (2010). *For Love of the Father: A Psychoanalytic Study of religious Terrorism*. Stanford, California: Stanford University Press.
Suzuki, D.T. (1949). *The Zen Doctrine of No-Mind: The Significance of the Sutra of Hui-Neng (Wei-Lang)*. London: Rider and Company.
Suzuki, D.T. (1964). *An Introduction to Zen Buddhism*. New York: Grove Press.
Taylor, C. (2002). *Varieties of Religion Today: William James Revisited*. Cambridge: Harvard University Press.
Taylor, C. (2007). *A Secular Age*. Cambridge: Cambridge University Press.
Thelen, K. and S. Steinmo (eds) (1992). *Structuring Politics: Historical Institutionalism in Comparative Perspective*. Cambridge: Cambridge University Press.
Tilly, C. (1975). *The Building of States in Western Europe*. Princeton: Princeton University Press.
Tipton, S. (1982). *Getting Saved from the Sixties: Moral Meaning in Conversion and Cultural Change*. Berkeley: University of California Press.
Von Laue, T.H. (1987). *The World Revolution of Westernization: The Twentieth Century in Global Perspective*. Oxford: Oxford University Press.
Wagner, P. (1994). *A Sociology of Modernity: Liberty and Discipline*. London: Routledge.
Wallerstein, I. (1974). *The Modern World System. Vol. I: Capitalist Agriculture and the Origins of the European World-Economy in the Sixteenth Century*. New York: Academic Press.
Ware, K. (1986). "The Hesychasts: Gregory of Sinai, Gregory Palamas, Nicolas Cabasilas" in C. Jones, G. Wainwright and E. Yarnold (eds). *The Study of Spirituality*. Oxford: Oxford University Press, 242-254.
Weber, M. (1925 [1978]). *Economy and Society. Vol. II*. Berkeley: University of California Press.
Wellman, B. (2002). "Little Boxes, Glocalisation and Networked Individualism" in M. Tanabe, P. van den Besselaar and T. Ishida (eds). *Digital Cities II*. Berlin: Springer-Verlag, pp. 11-25.
Williams, P. (1991). *Mahayana Buddhism: The Doctrinal Foundations*. London: Routledge.
Wilson, B.R. (1966). *Religion in a Secular Society: Fifty Years On*. London: Watts.
Wilson, B.R. (1982). *Religion in Sociological Perspective*. Oxford: Oxford University Press.
Wilson, B.R. (2001). 'Salvation, Secularization and De-Moralization' in R.K. Fenn (ed.). *The Blackwell Companion to Sociology of Religion*. Oxford: Blackwell, pp. 39-51.
Wolfenstein, E.V. (1997). "Hating the Self in the Other", *Journal for the Psychoanalysis of Culture and Society*, Vol. 2, No. 1.
Wuthnow, R. (1998). *After Heaven: Spirituality in America since the 1950s*. Berkeley: University of California Press.
Zizek, S. (2009). *Violence: Six Sideways Reflections*. London: Profile Books.
Zuckerman, P. (2009). "Atheism, Secularity and Well-Being: How the Findings of Social Science Counter Negative Stereotypes and Assumptions", *Sociology Compass*, Vol. 3, No. 6, pp. 949-971.

Index

A
adaptive capacity, 6, 12n24, 15
agnosticism, 74–75
Anderson, B., 5, 48
anthropocentrism, 72–73
anti-modernism, 41
anti-shah forces, 36
apatheism, 75–76
apophatism, 28, 28n11, 29, 56, 57, 59, 60–63, 73n3
Arab Spring movements, 37
atheism, 76–77
authoritarian-developmental modernity, 13–14

B
Basij organization, 36
Beck, Ulrich, 10n17, 74
belief systems, 3, 18, 28, 56
Besant, Annie, 63
Bourdieu, P., 90, 91, 93
Bruce, Steve, 21, 22
Buber, Martin, 56, 61, 65–69

    Buber-Levinas debate, 68–69
    I-it and the I-Thou relationship, 66
    relativism, issue of, 67

Buddhism, 92n8
Buddhist meditation techniques, 18

C
capitalism, 12, 15n29
Carnegie, Dale, 65
cataphatic, 27, 28, 60–63
Catholic Church, 71–72, 75
China, 13, 15n28, 50, 52
Christian dogmas, 18
Christian Europe, 78
Christian faith, 23, 24
Christianity, 20, 22, 23, 71, 72 christianization, 23
Christian orthodox theology, 56
communicative rationality, 66
Comte, Auguste, 51n7
conceptualisation, 85, 91
contextualisation, 41, 41n17, 43
cultural dimension, 34
cultural imperialism, 41, 50
cultural revolution, 37
cultural system, 88
Cupitt, Don, 27, 27n9

D

Dawkins, R., 21, 76
decision making, 63, 64
decision making
> dualism and strong voluntarism, 86–87
> dualism and weak voluntarism, 87–89
> dualism-duality dimension, 85
> duality and strong voluntarism, 92–93
> duality and weak voluntarism, 90–91
> voluntaristic dimension, 85

dedifferentiation, 37 democratization, global process of, 52 Dennet, D., 76
derationalization processes, 9, 10, 19
desecularization, 1, 22
detraditionalization, 25
dialectic, 1, 22–24, 22n4
drawing-in process, 5, 11
dualism, 87–89
> and strong voluntarism, 86–87
> and weak voluntarism, 87–89
> dualism-duality dimension, 85

duality
> and strong voluntarism, 92–93
> and weak voluntarism, 90–91
> duality-dualism dimension, 89

E

Eastern Orthodox Church, 59, 59n2
emotivism, 45, 54, 55, 58
encyclopaedia, 45
ethical issues, MacIntyre's theory, 44–47
> globalization, human rights and Euro-centrism issue, 49–51
> integration of practices, 47–49
> power structures and genealogy, 53–54
> sociocultural interpenetration, stepping stones towards, 51–53
> teleology and the unity of the narrative life, 54–57

Euro-centrism issue, 49–51
evangelical Christianity, 22
exclusive humanism, 26
expressive individualism, 25, 26
expressivist postsecular model, 22
extensive voting rights, 10
extreme nationalism, 41

F

faithless spirituality, 28
fanaticism, 38
Feuerbach, Later, 76, 80
Fink, B., 80, 80n1, 81
formal differentiation, 37
French monarchy, 4n3
Freudian perspective, fundamentalism, 39–41
fundamentalism, 33

cultural dimension, 34
fundamentalist phenomenon, specifity of, 33
psychodynamic dimension, 39–43
    Freudian perspective, 39–41
    Kleinian perspective, 41–42
    Lacanian perspective, 42–43
sociostructural dimension, 35–38
    national centre, inclusion into, 35–37
    top-down differentiation, 37
    widespread individualization, 38
fundamentalogenic pressures, 39, 40

G
genealogy, 53–54
Giddens, A., 25, 27, 29, 60, 61, 63n11, 73–75, 85
globalization, 49–51
globally-oriented practices, 49, 53
global mobilisation/inclusion, 8–99
global social differentiation, 9–10
global village, 37, 49
glocalisation, 49
God, 19, 27, 36, 59, 60, 71, 75, 92

H
Habermas' communicative theory, 62n10
Harris, S., 76
hesychasm, 28n11, 59, 73n3
heteronomous inclusion, 35
high Islam, 36
historical institutionalism, 87n4
homogenization, 7, 18
human rights, 49–51
Huxley, T.H., 74

I
I-it relationship, 66
imagined community, 1, 48, 52–54
inclusionary processes, 19, 29
indifference, 75n7
individualization, 24–29, 38
indwelling God, 73, 77
infrastructural powers, 5n6
institutional reflexivity, 65n14
institutional spheres, top-down differentiation of, 5–6, 19–24
instrumental rationality, 66
integration of practices, 47–49
interinstitutional dedifferentiation, 20
internal conversations, 88, 89

internal goods, 46
internal pacification, 24
internal reporting, 89
intra-institutional secularization, 21, 29, 72
Iran, 52
Islam, 36
islamisation, 37
I-Thou relationship, 66

J
jihad notion, 39
jouissance, 42

K
Kleinian perspective, fundamentalism, psychodynamic dimension, 41–42
Klein, Melanie, 39, 41–42
Krishnamurti, J., 28–29, 61, 63–65, 75

L
Lacanian perspective, fundamentalism, psychodynamic dimension, 42–43
Lacan, Jacques, 39, 79–84
    language, 80–83
    mysticism, 81–83
    symbolic, 80–81
    theory of language, 1

language, 80–83
late-late, 14, 14n26
Lau, C., 7
Leadbearer, C.W., 63
Levinas, E., 68–69
liberal democratic modernity, 12–13
liberalization, 21, 24, 26
liberal Protestantism, 72, 82
liberal spirituality, 24
Louis XIV France, 4

M

MacIntyre, Alasdair, 44–57 MacIntyre's theory, 44–47

    globalization, human rights and Euro-centrism issue, 49–51
    integration of practices, 47–49 power structures and genealogy, 53–54
    sociocultural interpenetration, stepping stones towards, 51–53
    teleology and the unity of the narrative life, 54–57

Mahayana Buddhism, 73
Martin, David, 22, 23, 25
Marx, Karl, 6, 19, 76
Mauss, Marcel, 18
McNeil, W. H., 13
Mead, G.H., 62n8
means of salvation, 36, 72
meditation, 1

    Lacan and

        language, 80–83
        mysticism, 81–83
        symbolic, 80–81

meditative thinking, 62n7
Mediterranean Europe, 51
Middle East, 37
Mill, J.S., 74
modernity

        and ethical issues

MacIntyre's theory, 44–57

      features, 3–4, 10–11
      fundamentalism, 33

    authoritarian-developmental modernity, 13–14
    concept of, 3
    decline of segmental localism and inclusion of the population, 4–5

        cultural dimension, 34
        fundamentalist phenomenon, specifity of, 33
        psychodynamic dimension, 39–43
        sociostructural dimension, 35–38

        global mobilisation/inclusion, 8–9
        global social differentiation, 9–10
        institutional spheres, top-down differentiation of, 5–6
        liberal democratic modernity, 12–13
        orientation

            agnosticism, 74–75
            anthropocentrism, 72–73
            apatheism, 75–76
            atheism, 76–77
            syncretism, 73–74
            theism, 71–72

        secularization, issue of, 19–24
        sociostructural features of, 29–31
        totalitarian modernity, 14–15
        widespread individualization, 6–7

        post-modern, 7–8

        religious trends individualization, 24–29
        religious rationalization, process of, 17–19

moral apatheism, 75
moral discourse, 52–54
Muslim Brotherhood, 37, 38
mysticism, 81–83

N
neo-evolutionist modernization theories, 10n19
New Age spiritualities, 23–, 26
new spiritualities, 24–29
New Testament, 79
Nitzschean/Foucauldian approach, 54
non differentiation, 37

O
orientation
    agnosticism, 74–75
    anthropocentrism, 72–73
    apatheism, 75–76
    atheism, 76–77
    syncretism, 73–74
    theism, 71–72
orthodox psychoanalytic method, 62–63

P
Parsonian theory, 87, 88
Parsons, Talcott, 6, 11n21, 12n24, 87
partial secularization, 20n3
patriotism, 48, 50
Pentecostal Christianity, 22
peripheralisation, 39

personality system, 88, 89
pluralistic party system, 10
polythetic adaptability, 90
population, inclusion of, 4–5
post-modern, 7–8
postsymbolic spirituality, 83
power structures, 53–54
procedural secularism, 72
progressivism, 24
projective identification process, 41n16
psychoanalysis, 56, 62, 81, 84
psycho-cultural, 3–4

Q
Qur'an, 20n3

R
racism, 41
radical apophatism, 63–65
rapid urbanization, 36
rational-choice institutionalism, 87, 87n4
rationality, 51–53
reflexive modernization theory, 60
reflexivity, 28n10, 60–63
relativism, issue of, 67
religious biography, 26
religious eclectivism, 74
religious fundamentalism, 34
religious rationalization, process of, 17–19
remagicalization, 19 Risse, T., 50
Robinson, J., 27

S
Sahn, Seung, 83
saintliness, 77
secularization, 1, 19–24
secularization-desecularization, 25
segmental localism, 4–5, 49, 72, 76
segmental organization, 38
self-actualization, 67, 68
self and self-other reflexivity, 57, 59
    apophatic and cataphatic, 60–63
    Buber, Martin, 65–69
        Buber-Levinas debate, 68–69
        I-it and the I-Thou relationship, 66
        relativism, issue of, 67
        radical apophatism, 63–65
self-self-relationship, 55–57, 60
Shermer, M., 76
shia tradition, 34
Sikkink, K., 50
social differentiation, 6, 14, 20, 29, 38
    global, 9–10
social structure, 33
societal transformation, 38
socio-cultural, 3
sociocultural interpenetration, stepping stones towards, 51–53
socio-historical contexts, 47
sociostructural, 1, 17
soft agnosticism, 75
Soviet Union, 12n24, 14, 14n27, 52

spiritual agnosticism, 75
spirituality, 24, 26–29, 63, 64, 75, 77–78, 82–84, 92n8 spiritual seeker, 27
Stein, Ruth, 39, 40
strong voluntarism, 92–93
structural-functional differentiation, 6, 19
structurationist approach, 91
substantive differentiation, 37
Suzuki, D.T., 83
symbolic, 80–81
symbolic castration, 42, 80
syncretism, 73–74

T
Taylor, Charles, 7n8, 21, 25–27, 29
teleology, 54–57 theism, 71–72
top-down differentiation, 37
    institutional spheres, 7, 13, 19–24
totalitarian modernity, 14–15
transcendental flourishing, 26
Turkey, 52

U
ultra-subjectivistic, 26
unconscious linguistic codes, 80
unity of the narrative life, 54–57
urban poverty, 41

V
violence, issues of, 42
voluntarism, 89–93
voluntaristic dimension, 85, 87

W
Wallerstein, Immanuel, 51–52
weak voluntarism, 87–91
Western Europe, 52
Western Europe atheism, 76
"white revolution," 40
widespread individualization, 6–7, 23, 25, 29, 30, 38
Wilson, Bryan, 25

Z
zealotism, 38
Zen Buddhism, 83
Zen Buddhist tradition, 62n7
Zizek, Slavoj, 42

www.ingramcontent.com/pod-product-compliance
Lightning Source LLC
Chambersburg PA
CBHW062027290426
44108CB00025B/2809